Taking Action in a Changing World

'The Great Being saith: Blessed and happy is he
that ariseth to promote the best interests
of the peoples and kindreds of the earth.'[1]
Bahá'u'lláh

'Service to humanity is service to God.'[2]
'Abdu'l-Bahá

To my parents, of course;
to Jadd, Eric and Mojan, and Lacey, for their constant support;
to Puran Stevens, for giving me so many examples
of integrity and courage in everyday life;
and especially to Alissa,
for far too many reasons to mention here

Taking Action

in a

Changing World

by

Aaron Emmel

George Ronald
Oxford

George Ronald, *Publisher*
www.grbooks.com

©Aaron Emmel 2005
All Rights Reserved

*A catalogue record for this book is available
from the British Library*

ISBN 0–85398–500–6

Cover: photograph by Joutiar Saleh
design by René Steiner

Printed in Great Britain
by Cromwell Press, Trowbridge

Contents

About the Author

Aaron Emmel works as an analyst and representative on human rights issues for a national organization. He has extensive experience with developing and managing projects in both business and non-profit environments and serves as a member of the Social Change Task Force of the Office of Development Research of the National Spiritual Assembly of the Bahá'ís of the United States. Aaron has written for dozens of publications and is the editor, with Heather Brandon, of the book *On the Front Lines*.

For discussions and more resources, visit Aaron at www.aaronemmel.com

Author's Note

I was assisted in the development of this manuscript by many experienced and knowledgeable people who generously answered my questions, sent me previously unpublished documents, and pointed me in useful directions. They include Peter Adriance, William Allmart, Elin Griffith, Dr Holly Hanson, Dr Mahnaz A. Javid, Christiana Lawson, Dr Cornell Menking, Layli Miller-Muro, Meghan Morris, Mojgan Sami, Sabine Schuller, Alissa Vancour, Soo-Jin Yoon and Laura Youngberg.

For making this book more readable, I owe a debt of gratitude to my editors, Dorrie Emmel, Elin Griffith, Christiana Lawson and Negin Toosi. I am also extremely grateful to my editor at George Ronald, Dr Wendi Momen.

I have learned a great deal from my collaborators on the Social Change Task Force of the Office of Development Research of the National Spiritual Assembly of the Bahá'ís of the United States, who include R. Weslie Ellison, Andra Grant, Elizabeth Herth, Celeste Nadeau, Michael Orona, Mojgan Sami, Alissa Vancour and Matthew Weinberg, as well, of course, as the Office's Director, William Allmart.

It should not be assumed that any of these people agree with anything in particular that I've written, nor should any of them be blamed for any of my mistakes. In addition, the quotations from Mojgan Sami represent her own opinions and not those of the World Bank Group, USAID or any of their partners, and the quotes of Sabine Schuller represent her own opinions and not those of the Rotary Foundation.

In all of the quotations used, I have tried to preserve the emphases and spelling of the originals.

Introduction

This book is based on a simple premise: People everywhere can create better material, emotional and spiritual lives for themselves.

The pages that follow are about social action. They're for people who want to leave the world a better place than they found it. Specifically, they're about ways to promote prosperity and justice.

Since social action is such a broad concept, this book has a focus: social and economic development projects. SED projects have the virtue of being immediately motivated by and directed at the need for social action and in one sense they're simply a way to translate a desire for social action into a sustainable form. Hopefully, however, it will soon become clear that the same concepts can be applied successfully to our businesses, our art workshops and our everyday lives.

Specifically, this book is meant to address one question. How do we turn our ideals into concrete actions that can improve the world? In other words, how do we get from the theories that we apply to other people in other places to the tools that can help all of us make a difference right here and right now?

To answer this question, *Taking Action* considers two sources of information. First, it's about the things people are doing at this moment, while you're reading this, to make the world a better place. Possibly, it's about some of the things you did yesterday or are planning on getting done this afternoon. Some of the things worked better than others; some of the things, in fact, haven't worked at all and they serve as good examples of what not to do. But they're all things that we can learn from.

Second, it's about those ideals that were just mentioned and how they relate to the real world and its challenges. Since I'm a

Bahá'í, I'm particularly interested in what the Bahá'í Faith has to say about contemporary issues.

This book is therefore an exploration of ways to apply Bahá'í principles and the teachings of other spiritual disciplines to social issues. It's not a book about the way Bahá'ís should understand these issues. To repeat, what follows is not a list of Bahá'í positions on various topics, nor is it meant to be.

This is the case for two reasons. First, because writing such a book would be impossible. This is explained by the Universal House of Justice:

> A Bahá'í scholar . . . will not make the mistake of regarding the sayings and beliefs of certain Bahá'ís at any one time as being the Bahá'í Faith. The Bahá'í Faith is the Revelation of Bahá'u'lláh: His Own Words as interpreted by 'Abdu'l-Bahá and the Guardian [Shoghi Effendi]. It is a revelation of such staggering magnitude that no Bahá'í at this early stage in Bahá'í history can rightly claim to have more than a partial and imperfect understanding of it.[3]

Second, this book draws from a wide variety of sources. Many of the people interviewed are not Bahá'ís. Many of the Bahá'ís who are interviewed have investigated different approaches to development and social action. Therefore it would be a mistake to presume that any part of this book speaks for Bahá'ís in general.

What follows is a look at how different people are determining which issues are important to them, how they're going about addressing them and how their initiatives are evolving into stable, long-lasting agencies of social change. Because it's about methods and approaches that are applicable in a variety of situations, it's not going to be able to answer every question – how to incorporate a non-profit organization, for example, which varies from country to country. With that said, *Taking Action* is intended to be used more as a handbook than a disquisition. Each chapter builds from the last and (I hope) contributes to a cohesive whole but it's also written in short sections so that you can put it down periodically and try out the things it talks about.

Every person who has been a Bahá'í for any length of time knows something about community development. The principles Bahá'ís try to apply in their daily lives are precisely those principles that are being singled out by international development agencies as crucial to the progress of populations. In the words of the Universal House of Justice, their engagement in Bahá'u'lláh's institutions ensures that 'the individual is not lost in the mass but becomes the focus of primary development, so that he may find his own place in the flow of progress, and society as a whole may benefit from the accumulated talents and abilities of the individuals composing it'.[4]

A Bahá'í has both the tools and the responsibility to help his or her community: he or she elects an assembly to guide it, reflects on its needs and critiques its performance at the monthly gatherings called 19 Day Feasts. The Bahá'í is called upon to excel at his or her education and career and develop his or her potential as a form of worship, to support the development of the community financially, to carry out the assembly's instructions and to serve on the assembly or one of its agencies if voted or appointed to the task. The assembly, in consultation with the community, sets goals for the future and tracks its progress along these benchmarks. These plans are designed to promote the goals of the national Bahá'í community, just as the national Bahá'í community's plans are designed to promote the goals of the global Bahá'í community. The community and the individual are not static; they are engaged in perpetual progress. This list can go on but these are some of the aspects of Bahá'í community life that spring most readily to mind. What this means is that the Bahá'í Faith is, in itself, a massive community development project.

Individual empowerment and initiative, universal education, participative decision-making, democratic processes, a scientific approach to solving problems, the harmonization of a person's inner and outer life – all of those terms and approaches so highly prized by development professionals – are a Bahá'í child's way of life by the time he or she turns 12. After teaching a number of Bahá'í children's classes, I'm confident that while children don't usually know the terms, many of them know how to make these ideas work and they can tell when they're absent.

A more recent development in the global Bahá'í community's efforts to apply Bahá'u'lláh's principles to everyday life is the study circle. Study circles are groups of people who come together to study the holy writings, promote recreational and cultural activities and engage in teaching and community service efforts. These study circles are designed to promote the organic development of individuals and communities by helping participants to learn and develop their own capacities, eventually becoming capable of going out and becoming tutors of new study circles themselves in an expanding process, with each study circle contributing to the health of the community through its actions of service.

These study circles are based on the power of the holy word; they are also, as Dr Peter Khan explained in a talk at the Bahá'í House of Worship in Sydney, Australia, in November 2003, about

> breaking down . . . the wall between clergy and congregation.
> Every religion up till now has had a congregation who basically sit
> there quietly, behave themselves, listen to their clergy and do what
> they are told. Bahá'u'lláh has come to break that down . . . We still
> tend to have hero-worship; we still tend to venerate certain indi-
> viduals rather than institutions and the like. It is not going to be
> easy; it is going to take us centuries to get out of our bloodstream
> the congregation vis-á-vis authority-individual kind of dynamic.
> The institutes and study circles are part of that dynamic.[5]

'One of the interesting things is the whole clustering activity going on in the Bahá'í world and what it does to neighbourhoods,' says Vasu Mohan, a development worker. 'Suddenly you start think-ing, who are the children in my neighbourhood who need virtues classes? Where in my neighbourhood can we hold devotional cir-cles? It's a paradigm shift. The scope of the activity, the primary target, is the neighbourhood.'[6]

For a Bahá'í, as Professor Holly Hanson points out in her book *Social and Economic Development*, development is a matter of applying Bahá'í principles to human life.[7] For those Bahá'ís interested in participating in community development, the essential theoretical grounding can be found in the letter of the Universal House of Justice of 20 October 1983 on this subject, as well as the 16 September 1993 statement from the Bahá'í World Centre called 'Bahá'í Social and Economic Development: Prospects for the Future'. Also essential reading is *The Prosperity of Humankind*, which was prepared by the Bahá'í International Community's Office of Public Information. Conveniently, these statements are gathered in the book *Readings on Bahá'í Social and Economic Development*, published in 2000 by Palabra Publications. Another important source, which contains the full text of the Universal House of Justice's October 1983 letter, is the book by Professor Hanson mentioned above, which is available from George Ronald, Publisher.

People interested in development work 'need to read the six principles that have been elaborated by the [Bahá'í Social and Economic Development] office in Haifa,' says Dr Mahnaz A. Javid, the president of the Mona Foundation, 'because they're based on decades of experience. Unless they understand and apply these principles, they're not going to be ultimately successful.'[8]

These principles are:

1) Degrees of complexity
2) Capacity building
3) Learning
4) Development of human resources
5) Influencing society
6) Integration

Point five, influencing society, involves a readiness to collaborate with individuals of capacity and leaders of thought in the application of Bahá'í teachings to the problems of society. The skills necessary to make this happen, according to 'Bahá'í Social and Economic Development: Prospects for the Future', are learned through action.

Ideas on how the Bahá'í teachings relate to current social problems and how we might apply them can be found below in chapters 1 to 3. The other five points are addressed, in a different order, in chapters 5 and 6.

Let's start with a look at five basic principles that can contribute to progress and prosperity and, to make sure they work, we'll consider them in light of some real-world challenges.

The Foundations of Development

The Crimson Book

We had a problem. There was a roomful of hungry teenagers and no food. A girl named Miriam and I, both recent high school graduates, tracked down the community centre's caretaker and asked him if we could use the phone to find out where lunch was.

'No phone today,' the caretaker said.

Miriam and I glanced at each other. There was a phone today. Unfortunately, it was in the half-closed drawer of the desk next to us. Right below the empty phone jack in the wall. 'Please,' I said. 'It's pretty important. There are a lot of hungry people resting on it.'

'No phone today.'

'We'll pay for the call,' Miriam offered.

'No phone today.'

'Can you please tell us why we can't use the phone?' I asked.

The caretaker was resolute. 'No phone today.'

Miriam and I were two of the organizers of a Bahá'í youth institute that was being held in this community centre in Belize City. Up until this point everything had been running pretty smoothly. I tried reasoning with the gentleman. 'We used the phone yesterday. Why can't we use the phone today?'

The caretaker's patience was not infinite. We had obviously exhausted it. '*No phone today.*'

'Yes, we got that, but could you please tell us *why*?'

'No phone today.'

'You see,' I said, 'we know there is a phone here. And we know that if we plug it back in it will work. So, since we know we can't use this phone, we would like to know why.'

'I've told you, no phone today.'

'Is there any particular reason for this?'

'It's Sunday,' he said.

Aha. Sunday. Well, of course. Religion was involved. It didn't have to make sense.

I learned several important lessons that day and not all of them were about the value youth place on lunch. They can be summarized like this: just because someone has a phone doesn't mean it's going to get used. Community development is primarily a spiritual and mental process, not a material one. If we're going to look at how people use their resources and why they make the choices they do, we'll have to consider their mental models of the world and this is an area in which religion plays a major role.

Ideally, of course, religion should not only make sense, it should cultivate our capacity to imagine, investigate and explore. But it's a powerful force. It can be used for enormous good and terrible evil. We can probably all come up with examples of both. One of the things that makes religion so pivotal in development is that, like any ideology, it offers people a vision of something larger than what's visible in front of them. And that has to happen before anyone can decide to work for social change.

The world's great spiritual traditions motivate. They inspire people to serve a good larger than their own immediate needs. Indiana University's Center on Philanthropy Panel Study has found that a person who has a religion is more likely to contribute to charities than someone who doesn't. If they both give, the religious person is likely to give more.[1]

Another study, of villagers in Iran, identified a link between education and association with the Bahá'í Faith: 'the higher the level of education of the Bahá'ís, the higher the degree of religiosity and the lower the number of children'.[2] That's because, at its best, religion doesn't just encourage us to develop ourselves and our communities, it gives us the tools to do so. When we commit to spiritual development, by definition we're committing to the

fulfilment of our innate potential. This is all good to keep
because otherwise what comes next might sound hyperbolic: by
applying certain spiritual principles we can make this a better
world.

The secret to prosperity can be found in Bahá'u'lláh's writings:
'Unveiled and unconcealed, this Wronged One hath, at all times,
proclaimed before the face of all the peoples of the world that
which will serve as the key for unlocking the doors of sciences, of
arts, of knowledge, of well-being, of prosperity and wealth.'[3]

In the Tablet of the World, revealed in Haifa, Palestine, in
1891,[4] Bahá'u'lláh indicates that prosperity should be one of the
aims of a country's laws:

> Give ear unto that which, if heeded, will ensure the freedom, well-
> being, tranquillity, exaltation and advancement of all men. Certain
> laws and principles are necessary and indispensable for Persia.
> However, it is fitting that these measures should be adopted in
> conformity with the considered views of His Majesty – may God
> aid him through His grace – and of the learned divines and of
> the high-ranking rulers. Subject to their approval a place should
> be fixed where they would meet. There they should hold fast to
> the cord of consultation and adopt and enforce that which is con-
> ducive to the security, prosperity, wealth and tranquillity of the
> people.[5]

Bahá'u'lláh identifies at least five principles as being conducive to
'advancement' and 'reconstruction':

> Whilst in the Prison of 'Akká, We revealed in the Crimson Book[6]
> that which is conducive to the advancement of mankind and to
> the reconstruction of the world. The utterances set forth therein
> by the Pen of the Lord of creation include the following which
> constitute the fundamental principles for the administration of
> the affairs of men:
>   First: It is incumbent upon the ministers of the House of
> Justice to promote the Lesser Peace so that the people of the earth

may be relieved from the burden of exorbitant expenditures. This matter is imperative and absolutely essential, inasmuch as hostilities and conflict lie at the root of affliction and calamity.

Second: Languages must be reduced to one common language to be taught in all the schools of the world.

Third: It behoveth man to adhere tenaciously unto that which will promote fellowship, kindliness and unity.

Fourth: Everyone, whether man or woman, should hand over to a trusted person a portion of what he or she earneth through trade, agriculture or other occupation, for the training and education of children, to be spent for this purpose with the knowledge of the Trustees of the House of Justice.

Fifth: Special regard must be paid to agriculture. Although it hath been mentioned in the fifth place, unquestionably it precedeth the others. Agriculture is highly developed in foreign lands, however in Persia it hath so far been grievously neglected. It is hoped that His Majesty the Sháh – may God assist him by His grace – will turn his attention to this vital and important matter.[7]

The Importance of Agriculture

That agriculture is linked to societal advancement should not be surprising. The development of agriculture is, after all, generally seen as coinciding with the development of civilization. A society's stability and prosperity rest squarely on its ability to feed its people and people who are hungry will be hard pressed to develop themselves economically and socially. 'When children are sick or hungry', Dr Javid points out, 'you cannot educate them.'[8]

Eight hundred million people don't get enough food to eat but don't let that number fool you: the problem is much bigger than that. Two billion don't get enough iodine, which is important for a healthy brain.[9] Four and a half billion people suffer from iron deficiency, which leads to fatigue, shortness of breath and lethargy. This contributes to a decline of productivity that is said to decrease some countries' gross domestic products by two per cent. About half of the children in developing countries seem to suffer

4

from cognitive impairments owing to a lack of iron, with an average loss, says a scientist at the United Nations University in New Hampshire, of five to ten IQ points.[10]

For this reason helping people to feed themselves is a primary goal of community development projects all across the world. At Rabbani Bahá'í School in the state of Madhya Pradesh in India students are taught how to raise crops at the same time that they learn mathematics and language. At the Ruaha Secondary School in Iringa, operated by the National Spiritual Assembly of the Bahá'ís of Tanzania and one of the many projects that the Mona Foundation supports, students take courses in animal husbandry. Not every development project needs to focus on farming methods, of course, but all other material advances are based on people's ability to feed and otherwise sustain themselves from their environments.

In his Pulitzer Prize-winning book *Guns, Germs, and Steel*, Dr Jared Diamond develops the intriguing theory that differences in the agricultural potential of different regions were responsible for differences in the complexity and organization of their societies and are ultimately behind the geopolitics of the present day. Whether or not this is the case, the link between agriculture and progress in the modern age is indisputable.

In 19th century England, which saw agricultural productivity grow at a rate of about one per cent a year starting at about 1800, agricultural advances and the industrial revolution were inseparable and mutually reinforcing.[11]

The 20th century's Green Revolution quite plainly changed the world. This confluence of agricultural innovations led to the introduction of petroleum-based fertilizers, which increased crop yields by infusing the soil with nitrogen, the introduction of herbicides and pesticides which raised productivity in the 1940s and 1950s and the increased use of tractors and other farm machines. Between the second decade of the century and the close of the 1960s America raised its rice yield from 4.25 to nearly 12 tons per acre.

The Green Revolution also changed the world's demographics by transferring people from rural areas to cities. The rural–urban shift had at least two causes: farmers were driven out of work by the fact that the agricultural revolution's capital-intensive techniques favoured large businesses and the increases in food production made it possible to sustain the large numbers of people who went to the cities because that's where the jobs were.

Modern farming techniques have also sustained the world's economic disparities. In the second half of the 20th century, Russia, India and China – all major grain producers – found themselves importing American wheat because the Americans could produce it more cheaply. As this indicates, the countries that have the most urgent need for agricultural advances have also usually been the countries which lacked the resources to take advantage of them.[12] The way we farm has other economic and political consequences as well, such as the world's reliance on fossil fuels: by 1974, the average US farm required one calorie of fossil energy to produce one calorie of food energy.[13]

Because so many of us live in cities (47 per cent by the year 2000 and a projected 58 per cent by 2025[14]), it's easy to forget the crucial role that agriculture plays in our lives as a primary driver of material society. Agriculture is one of the core factors of economic prosperity and plays a role in social and political structures as well. In chapter 3, we'll look at the importance of targeting core issues in our attempts to affect social change; on a country-wide level, no analysis of core issues can be complete unless it considers the production and distribution of food.

However, there's something intriguing about how Bahá'u'lláh introduces the concept of agriculture in the passage above. He lists five points and says that agriculture is the most important – but He positions it last. Now, I have no idea why it's listed last. What I do know is that it is. Which means that we're already thinking about the other four principles by the time we get to the part about agriculture. And once we reflect on it, it will become clear that even though the development of agriculture is essential for a healthy humanity, agriculture can't reach its full potential unless the other four principles are also being applied. Quite simply, material means are not the basis of material prosperity. In Bahá'u'lláh's words: 'When the eyes of the people of the East were captivated by the arts and wonders of the West, they roved distraught in the wilderness of material causes, oblivious of the One Who is the Causer of Causes . . .'[15]

For example, just now we saw how well the United States did from the Green Revolution. But the Green Revolution wasn't created for the United States. In 1944 the Rockefeller Foundation founded an institute to improve the agricultural output of Mexican farms. It worked. In 1944 Mexico imported half its wheat; in 1964 it was a wheat exporter.[16] In the 1960s the programme was expanded to Pakistan and India. Pakistan went from producing 4.6 million tons of wheat in 1965 to 12.3 million tons in 1970. India went from producing 12.3 million tons of wheat in 1965 to 20 million tons in 1970.[17]

The Green Revolution worked because it applied the spiritual principles of education and investigation to a pressing problem: the scarcity of food. Just as importantly, it worked because it recognized the interconnectedness of humanity, which is the major theme running through the four points above, and brought together scientists from different countries to work on problems that affected people they probably had never seen before.[18] One of the reasons the United States benefited so much from the Green Revolution was that it already had the technology, wealth and infrastructure to take advantage of it. It also profited, though, because by helping to create tools that could be used abroad, its researchers developed strategies that could also be applied domestically. When the Rockefeller Foundation decided to make a difference in Mexico, the world's interdependence ensured that it was also going to make a difference at home.

Actually, by applying the principles listed above we can start addressing some of the factors that lead to food scarcity before we even begin thinking about what we're planting in the ground.

So far, no country with democracy and a free press has ever suffered a famine, regardless of how rich or poor it is. The reasons that are usually suggested for this are that a free press will alert people to potential disasters before famines start and representative governments know that they will be held accountable for any failures to take appropriate action.[19] Representative governments and an open method of communication are implied in the four points Bahá'u'lláh lists before agriculture, as we'll see below, but just in case we don't get the connection, He mentions them both explicitly elsewhere. For instance, on the subject of the press, Bahá'u'lláh declares that journalists and editors 'should enquire into situations as much as possible and ascertain the facts, then set them down in writing'.[20]

What if we're growing enough food and our countries are well-governed? People still might not be getting enough to eat unless they're becoming educated. In this context, it's particularly important to focus on the education of women. Lisa Smith and Lawrence Haddad of the International Food Policy Research Institute in Washington DC studied 63 countries and found that between 1970 and 1995, improvements in women's education and life expectancy relative to men helped to reduce the proportion of children who were malnourished by 50 per cent.[21]

By now it should be clear that these five principles can't be entirely understood in isolation. So let's move on to the next one.

The Lesser Peace and International Security

The world's social and economic development is hampered by military expenditures. In the words of 'Abdu'l-Bahá, the son of Bahá'u'lláh and authorized interpreter of His teachings, 'the whole world is distressed because of the excessive burden and irreparable damage of war. Taxes are levied to meet its drain. Every year the burden increases . . .'[22]

One researcher, Ruth Sivard, asserted in the 1970s that less than one per cent of the world's annual arms budget would have been enough to teach everyone in the world to read and write. Less than two per cent could have paid for education for the 50 per cent of third-world children who didn't have the opportunity to go to school. Exactly one per cent would have provided clean water for the two billion people who lacked it.[23]

8

Of course, warfare and other forms of violence also have more direct social costs. The amount of human suffering caused by warfare is almost too vast for comprehension. By 2003, 2,500 people were dying in the war in the Democratic Republic of Congo every day. Somewhere between 3.3 and 4.7 million people had been killed in the struggle since 1998, most of them not during battle but from starvation and illness caused by the disruption of the country's infrastructure.[24]

The Lesser Peace refers to a political peace that is enforced by the nations of the world. Trends towards a collective commitment to peace began in the 20th century.

These trends have not been driven, in the main, by idealism. They have been propelled instead by humanity's stubborn will to survive. The Universal House of Justice put the choice plainly in its 1985 statement *The Promise of World Peace*: 'Whether peace is to be reached only after unimaginable horrors precipitated by humanity's stubborn clinging to old patterns of behaviour, or is to be embraced now by an act of consultative will, is the choice before all who inhabit the earth.'[25] So far the world has chosen unimaginable horrors. Or, as Austro-Hungarian Count Czernin put it after the First World War: 'We had to die. But we could choose the means of our death, and we chose the most terrible.'[26]

In parliament buildings, presidential palaces, newsrooms and town halls all over the world we're clinging to old patterns of behaviour that can be described, as a generalization, as unjust and provincial. But technology and a host of other factors have made injustice unsustainable and the world is now interconnected. Old patterns of behaviour no longer work and their failure can be tallied with body counts.

To return to the words of the Universal House of Justice, this time on the topic of the decades-long attempt of the Islamic Republic of Iran to exterminate the country's indigenous Bahá'í community:

Ruling elites can make no more serious error than to imagine that the power they have managed to arrogate to themselves provides an enduring bulwark against the relentless tides of historical change. Today, in Iran as everywhere throughout the world, these tides roll in with insistent urgency and tumultuous force. They are not merely at the door of the house, but rise up irresistibly through its floors. They cannot be diverted. They cannot be denied . . . This is the real reason why Bahá'u'lláh was so desperately opposed by clergy and rulers who recognized in Him – correctly if only dimly – the Voice of a coming society of justice and enlightenment, in which they themselves would have no place.[27]

Although the Universal House of Justice indicated in 1985 that we did indeed have a choice, Shoghi Effendi, the Bahá'í Faith's Guardian, had already predicted the route we would take before settling on consultation. 'We have but to turn our gaze to humanity's blood-stained history to realize that nothing short of intense mental as well as physical agony has been able to precipitate those epoch-making changes that constitute the greatest landmarks in the history of human civilization,' he wrote in a 1931 letter to the American Bahá'ís.[28]

The political history of the 20th century is the story of a world rejecting Bahá'u'lláh's prescriptions for peace and then having them forced upon it incrementally by ever-increasing crises. The more firmly we reject Bahá'u'lláh's principles, the more terrors pile up before they are finally adopted.

On 5 December 1912, aboard the steamship *Celtic* that would take Him to England on His way back to the Holy Land, 'Abdu'l-Bahá warned the Bahá'ís: 'Consider what is happening in the Balkans. Human blood is being shed, properties are destroyed, possessions pillaged, cities and villages devastated. A world-enkindling fire is astir in the Balkans.'[29] Two years later, World War I erupted in the Balkans.

In 1815 participants of the Congress of Vienna established a 'concert of Europe' that relied on a balance of the power of the most powerful states on the continent to keep Europe out of wars. This system lasted until about 1870 and the Franco-Prussian War.

The Franco-Prussian War was part of an effort by Prussia to

forge a stronger nation and out of it emerged a unified Germany. In the decades that followed, European countries sought to prevent attacks by their neighbours by forging alliances with other powers.

This network of alliances backfired and, in fact, accelerated the plunge into World War I. When Austria–Hungary used the assassination of Archduke Franz Ferdinand by a member of an internal Serbian nationalistic organization as an excuse to declare war against Serbia, despite Serbia's attempts to cooperate with Austria–Hungary's demands for justice, Russia mobilized in defence of its Slavic cousins in Serbia. Germany mobilized to defend Austria–Hungary against Russia. France mobilized in response to Germany's mobilization. Germany attacked Belgium to reach France before France could strike Germany. England joined the war to defend Belgium and attack the Ottoman Empire, a new German ally, to prevent Germany from seizing the continent.

The world was not prepared for the technologies of destruction unleashed by the new war. Europe was devastated and Asia suffered tremendously. The first major war in Europe since 1815 changed the art, literature, economy, thinking, and social and political systems of the continent.

So, in the aftermath of World War I, the League of Nations was created to lead to the end of war. It was established in 1920, thanks to the activism of President Woodrow Wilson, but the US Senate never ratified the treaty and the United States never joined. The League of Nations was to develop a framework for arbitration between disputing parties to avoid armed conflict. It was to encourage nations to willingly disarm. And it was to coordinate collective security to prevent any nation from rising up against another.

It sounded great on paper but it had no power of enforcement and no power of will. By the time the unresolved tensions of World War I erupted into World War II, the League had repeatedly proved its own irrelevancy and inadequacy.

What was behind all this conflict? Why did the human race seem incapable of breaking out of its cycle of wars?

To many people, there's no point in even asking this question. War, they would say, is human nature; in fact, it's even more primal than human nature because it's an act engaged in by all higher primates. On the other hand, what is civilization but the result of people's willingness to trust and cooperate? And even someone who feels that war is inevitable has to admit that there are certain conditions in which conflict is likelier than others.

Those conditions were explained by Bahá'u'lláh, and 'Abdu'l-Bahá repeated them throughout His 1912 tour of the United States. The most pressing problems facing the human race, 'Abdu'l-Bahá said, were based on people's failure to acknowledge the basic one-ness of humanity. Specifically, we needed to end racial, national and all other types of prejudice; women and men needed to be recognized as equals; and an end to economic disparity needed to be found through the application of spiritual principles. 'This readjustment of the social economy is of the greatest importance inasmuch as it ensures the stability of the world of humanity,' He stated.[30]

Compare these standards with the situation that led to World War II. Obviously, the political scene was male-dominated. Both racial and patriotic prejudice was appealed to: 'For myself and all other true National-Socialists there is only one doctrine: Nation and Fatherland. What we have to fight for is security for the exist-ence and increase of our race and our nation...'[31] In their rise to power, the Nazis exploited widespread frustrations arising from the economic tensions of the Great Depression and what Germans perceived as unfair financial burdens imposed by the Treaty of Versailles.

The principles that 'Abdu'l-Bahá articulated in 1912 and the vision of collective security that Bahá'u'lláh announced prior to that in the prison of 'Akká have been implemented with increasing degrees of urgency ever since. As we've seen above, this hasn't been because people have been idealistic. It hasn't even happened be-cause they've generally known what the principles are. It's because the principles are necessary for our security and progress – a lesson we've been learning through trial and a whole lot of error.

The leaders of every nation-state want sovereignty but sovereignty is threatened when a nation's borders can be invaded by its neighbours. And many leaders want power but, most of all, people want to survive. And when the world is drowning in blood, people inevitably find the price for survival and they pay it. While World War II still raged, US President Franklin D. Roosevelt and British Prime Minister Winston Churchill vowed that if the Allies won they would form an organization which would, as the United Nation's charter declares, 'save succeeding generations from the scourge of war, which twice in our lifetime has brought untold sorrow to mankind'. Each state had its own private agenda for joining, of course. But the result was that in 1945, in San Francisco, the United Nations was formally established.

Two global wars had forced people into recognizing the necessity of international consultation. They had moved a step closer to the type of assembly anticipated by Bahá'u'lláh: 'The time must come when the imperative necessity for the holding of a vast, an all-embracing assemblage of men will be universally realized. The rulers and kings of the earth must needs attend it, and, participating in its deliberations, must consider such ways and means as will lay the foundations of the world's Great Peace among men.'[32]

The United Nations did not end war in 1945, of course. What it did do was provide a global forum for discussion, a fundamental prerequisite of peace. One of the things the United Nations lacked was the ability to carry out the rest of Bahá'u'lláh's statement: 'Should any king take up arms against another, all should unitedly arise and prevent him.'[33]

After up to 100,000 people had died in what Madeleine Albright dubbed 'Africa's first world war' in the Democratic Republic of Congo, the United Nations Security Council in 2000 committed 5,500 troops and 37 observers to enforce a ceasefire. Jocelyn Coulon of Toronto's *The Globe and Mail* explained the realities of the situation:

So, what will the peacekeepers do? According to the U.N. resolution adopted Feb. 24, they will oversee the ceasefire and help the

13

parties fulfil their obligations under the Lusaka accord. However, they do not have a mandate to disarm the combatants, never mind to take military action against those who violate the accord. In fact, the peacekeepers essentially depend on signatories' good will to keep their word.[34]

This situation is similar to one facing the UN all over the world. Conflicts which disrupt countries and sometimes involve entire regions demand UN intervention. But the UN can only come when asked, must convince member states to commit troops and then can only use the troops as little more than human shields once they are installed – they interpose themselves between the former combatants and can only use their weapons in self-defence. In short, the UN has no power to fulfil one of its most important functions.

It is not surprising, then, that the United States has long been at the forefront of the collective action that's increasingly taking place on the world stage. This is a role 'Abdu'l-Bahá called on it to perform when He visited the country in 1912:

> Therefore, it is my hope that you may stand forth as the first herald of peace and hoist this banner, for this banner will be hoisted . . . Just now Europe is a battlefield of ammunition ready for a spark, and one spark will set aflame the whole world. Before these complications and cataclysmic events happen, take the step to prevent it.[35]

The United States missed its chance in 1912. But it has tried to make up for the lapse more recently. For example, during the Bosnian crisis of the 1990s the UN Security Council refused to get involved. But the North Atlantic Treaty Organization, led by the United States, did.

However, it's neither possible nor desirable for one country to safeguard the entire planet. It runs the risk of exhausting its immediate resources, alienating and frightening its international neighbours and encountering conflicts between its domestic obligations and international imperatives.

As has happened at every step along the way, it was bloodshed that precipitated calls for the United Nations to move closer to Bahá'u'lláh's vision of the Lesser Peace. Events in East Timor and Sierra Leone in the 1990s helped to convince many observers that the United Nations needed to be given stronger peacekeeping powers.

Sierra Leone, an African nation of four million people, collapsed into a civil war in 1991 which resulted in at least 10,000 people having their hands chopped off, at least 50,000 being killed and two million being displaced. The United Nations sent in peacekeepers. Sierra Leone's Revolutionary United Front kidnapped hundreds of these peacekeepers and threw the entire mission into chaos. The UN force might have been driven away entirely except for the timely arrival of British troops. Responding to the United Nations's lack of preparedness for dealing with conflict, Paris's *Le Monde* stated, 'The West cannot do everything. It cannot intervene militarily everywhere, which, moreover, would be poorly viewed for other reasons. In the face of this objective limit, there are only two possibilities: Either the U.N. delegates to others, or we equip it with the proper military means.'[36]

Additional reforms will have to take place in the Security Council. The United Nations Security Council is responsible for maintaining peace in the world in accordance with the UN's principles. One of its powers is the authority to take military action against an aggressor. Every other organ of the United Nations may only make recommendations to national governments. But under the United Nations Charter, all member countries agree to accept and carry out the Security Council's decisions. In theory, then, the world's nations are bound by the Security Council's decisions.

The Council is composed of 15 member countries. Five are permanent members and the remaining ten are elected by the UN General Assembly for two-year terms. Decisions on procedural matters require assenting votes by at least nine of the 15 members. Decisions on substantive matters require at least nine votes, including either concurring votes or abstentions from all five permanent members: the United States, China, France, Russia and the

United Kingdom. This is the rule of 'great power unanimity': the world's great powers as they were recognized at the end of World War II have to unanimously agree for the Security Council to take a stand against a country. In effect, this gives all of the permanent members a 'veto power' because each of them can veto an action simply by voting in the negative.

There are two striking features of this arrangement. First, an agency for enforcing international law already exists. Second, the veto power renders it subject to the influence of five powers, any one of which may not have the best interests of the rest of the world in mind and any one of which can render the body powerless to act in any way that threatens its own self-interest. This is not consistent with collective decision-making and it curtails collective action. The veto power, for example, is the reason why NATO, and not the United Nations, intervened in Bosnia in the 1990s.

As in every other arena, however, the Security Council is moving in the direction of greater international cooperation. As this book is being written, the United Nations is discussing reforms that would expand Security Council membership, and Brazil, Germany, India and Japan are all pressing for permanent seats on the institution.

The Bahá'í International Community issued a statement called *Turning Point for All Nations* in 1995, on the fiftieth anniversary of the establishment of the UN. Part of it reads:

> In its 1955 submission on UN reform, the Bahá'í International Community argued for the gradual elimination of the concepts of 'permanent membership' and 'veto power' as confidence in the Security Council would build. Today, forty years later, we reaffirm that position. However, we also propose that, as a transitionary step, measures be introduced to curb the exercise of the veto power to reflect the original intention of the Charter.[37]

In the same document the Bahá'í International Community states that a representative government and a commitment to human rights should be minimum requirements for participation in the UN General Assembly.[38]

Recognition of humanity's interconnectedness doesn't just need to be achieved by presidents and ministers. It's vital knowledge for anyone interested in initiating positive social change.

In 2004 I asked Mojgan Sami, an operations analyst in the Social Development Department of the World Bank, what was lacking in present-day community development. Her answer: a sense of mutual responsibility and accountability.

'It is no longer possible in our world to believe that one nation's development happens in isolation,' Sami explains. 'Without a change in the attitude of the community of nations towards social and economic development, we will not be able to achieve sustainable global prosperity. Development is linked to trade, conflict, equality, availability of natural resources, politics, education, corporate social responsibility, etc. Unless and until the community of nations realize these critical/complex linkages and learn to adapt policies to enable countries to achieve their own prosperity, we will not be able to step out of the poverty trap.'[39]

This assertion is confirmed by 'Trade Policy and Global Poverty,' a 2004 study by William Cline, a senior fellow at the Washington-based Center for Global Development and the Institute for International Economics. The study looks at trade barriers, which countries put in place in order to protect their own economies from those of other countries. According to the study, eliminating global trade tariffs and other protective barriers would lift at least 500 million people out of poverty over 15 years. Developing countries would realize long-term economic benefits of about $200 billion a year. Industrialized nations would be able to convey about twice as much economic benefit to developing countries as they currently provide through foreign aid but at a benefit rather than a cost to their own consumers.[40]

A Common Language

As part of the research for her Master's thesis, Marcella LeFever interviewed a Hmong Bahá'í who had entered the United States as a teenage refugee. His first impressions of America were filtered through the loneliness that comes from not knowing the native language: 'Everything was just so completely strange, for the first month we were completely lost . . . It was just very scary. You don't understand anybody. You don't know whether they're saying positive or negative things.' He had to learn how to communicate all over again. 'At high school everybody used a lot of slang and cussing. It took three months to understand anything that was going on and get used to the language . . . Everyone [in my family] was homesick. Everyone wanted to go back.'

But once he was able to understand others and make himself understood, he thrived. 'I graduated in 1991 as co-valedictorian . . . Then I went . . . for my Masters in Information Technology.'[41]

Bahá'u'lláh's call for the adoption of a common language is intended to help people communicate with each other more easily and is thus one of the developments that 'will promote fellowship, kindliness and unity':[42]

> In former Epistles We have enjoined upon the Trustees of the House of Justice either to choose one language from among those now existing or to adopt a new one, and in like manner to select a common script, both of which should be taught in all the schools of the world. Thus will the earth be regarded as one country and one home.[43]

Helping people to communicate with each other has immediate benefits. In the early 1980s, when the Persian Affairs Committee of the National Spiritual Assembly of the Bahá'ís of the United States asked Persian Bahá'ís around the country to name some of the challenges they faced, a recurring response was that people who had been doctors or teachers in Iran felt frustrated with the fact that in the United States, because they weren't fluent in English, their opinions weren't heard or, if they were heard, they weren't taken seriously.

In 2003, when the Spiritual Assembly of the Bahá'ís of Dallas, Texas, was looking for ways to help Persian Bahá'í immigrants and refugees feel more connected to community life and build new material futures for themselves, one of their strategies was to encourage American-born Bahá'ís to teach the newcomers English-language skills.

The world's seemingly intractable problems are exacerbated by the barriers people face in their attempts to communicate. When Middle Easterners took to the streets in 2001 to protest the United States's invasion of Afghanistan, it was partly because many of them had been misinformed that Israeli pilots had flown the planes into New York's World Trade Center and they didn't understand why, if that were the case, the US would attack the Taliban. The US Congress responded to its seeming inability to communicate with the Arab world by starting an Arabic-language satellite TV channel based in Virginia, Al Hurra, which went live in February 2004.

The same stories can play differently in different parts of the world, as one writer observed in *The Atlantic Monthly* in 2004: 'In August, when I left on one of my visits to Iran, a media blitz at home was trumpeting a more or less nonstop parade of American triumphs in the Olympic Games in Greece. Days later in Tehran the popular press was heralding a humiliating cascade of US defeats.'[44]

When people learn about each other indirectly, the results can be disastrous. If you'd read *Ha'aretz* in Tel Aviv in 2001, you'd have learned that Palestinian Authority leader 'Arafat covered his ears to avoid hearing . . . calls of mercy. He also covered his ears to block out the voice of wisdom telling him that Ehud Barak has turned over every stone in the search for a much-desired peace . . .' But if you read *Al-Rai* in Amman, you'd have discovered that 'Whenever Israel finds itself in political turmoil, it resorts to threatening Arab capitals with military force. No matter what, it tries to change the rules of the game of politics when it is likely that it will lose . . .'[45] With the information that both groups were receiving about each other seeming to share no objective reference points, it's not surprising that they had difficulty trusting each other.

Advances in media technology are breaking down mental barriers that have been sustained by poor communication. People from different countries can learn about each other on TV and chat with each other on the Internet. They're building virtual connections through websites and email. As a result, they're finding themselves identifying with people and becoming concerned about events that in the past they might not have spent much time thinking about. Media technology is making it more difficult for us to ignore crises just because they occur somewhere else.

Communication technologies helped people across the world feel connected in December 2004 when a tsunami in the Indian Ocean left hundreds of thousands dead. During its annual new year's celebration, Australia led the world in a global minute of silence. On the Champs Elysees in Paris trees were shrouded in black. In Illinois, where I lived at the time, a baker I was buying bread from spoke with distress about the situation and said that he was planning a fund-raiser that weekend to raise money for survivors. We were on the other side of the world but through TV, newspapers and the Internet we were united.

When Bahá'u'lláh spoke about an international community, the nature of the society He expressed was physically impossible. It took months for people to circle the globe. Yet the beginning of a technologically connected world began on the very first day of the Bahá'í Era. On the day following the Báb's declaration of His mission as Bahá'u'lláh's forerunner and the bringer of a new revelation from God, Samuel F. B. Morse sent the first telegraph message: 'What hath God wrought?' Before this, the fastest means of communication had been smoke signals and similar technologies or a rider on a swift horse. On 24 May 1844 a new age began. In his book *The Lexus and the Olive Tree*, Thomas L. Friedman, the foreign affairs correspondent for *The New York Times*, demonstrates that the era of globalization began in the middle of the 19th century.[46]

Shoghi Effendi very clearly links technology with future progress, in both communication and society: 'A mechanism of world intercommunication will be devised, embracing the whole planet, freed from national hindrances and restrictions, and functioning with marvellous swiftness and perfect regularity,' he wrote in 1936.[47]

Such technology facilitates worldwide consultation and makes possible the type of press that Shoghi Effendi asserts must inherit the world's media:

> The press will . . . while giving full scope to the expression of the diversified views and convictions of mankind, cease to be mischievously manipulated by vested interests, whether private or public, and will be liberated from the influence of contending governments and peoples.[48]

In the state of Illinois, the Department of Human Services formed a Refugee Social Services Consortium of refugee advocacy organizations to help procure bilingual, community-based services for refugees and immigrants. The department knew that the more quickly refugees were able to understand the options available to them and communicate their needs, the more quickly they would be able to become self-sufficient. It hoped that community refugee organizations could help them reach that goal.

Once a month the Consortium hosts a meeting for representatives of community-based organizations that work with immigrants and refugees. At the May 2004 meeting participants were asked to engage in a simple exercise. They were told to think of some small action that could be realistically implemented and which, if practised, would make a significant difference in their day-to-day work.

Many of the representatives there – some of them the directors of their organizations, with decades of experience – said that they were able to make the biggest impact on behalf of the refugees they advocated for when they were able to tell other members of the community who these refugees were, the challenges they faced and the places they came from. They felt that if they could find better ways to build bridges of communication between these diverse groups of people – the refugees and the native residents of Illinois – it would help their organizations to raise funds, solicit volunteers and change state legislation. There's a straightforward reason for this, they explained: we're willing to do a lot more for people when we know their stories.

For those of us interested in social action, this raises some interesting questions. How can we help people to communicate for themselves so that they can navigate their environments and obtain what they need without having to continue to rely on our help? How can we make it easier for people from different backgrounds to communicate with each other? How many of the conflicts we want to alleviate are due to a lack of communication?

The Promotion of Fellowship, Kindliness and Unity

One of the best ways to ensure progress is to help people build bonds of fellowship. This principle is absolutely essential to any discussion of development, so it's worth spending some time on it.

Unity and fellowship, of course, are the bedrock of Bahá'u'lláh's Revelation:

> The distinguishing feature that marketh the pre-eminent character of this Supreme Revelation consisteth in that We have, on the one hand, blotted out from the pages of God's holy Book whatsoever hath been the cause of strife, of malice and mischief amongst the children of men, and have, on the other, laid down the essential prerequisites of concord, of understanding, of complete and enduring unity.[49]

The relationship between 'the essential prerequisites of concord' and social and economic development has been demonstrated over and over again since the 19th century when those words were revealed. For example, one of these fundamental prerequisites is the abolition of racial prejudice. The government of South Africa, which institutionalized racial prejudice through the system of apartheid, discovered in the 1990s that the system was economically unsustainable. Apartheid ended without a revolution not simply because the white rulers had a change of heart, although some of them did, but because the more grossly a society rejects the principles of concord, the more difficult it is to sustain.

One of the reasons for apartheid's demise was that it relied on a black majority which was poor and under-educated, allowing factory and other business owners to exploit them as a source of cheap, mobile and malleable labour. What the government eventually found out was that if most of the population is made up of people who are underpaid, there aren't going to be enough people with enough money to buy all the goods those underpaid people are producing. As people around the world started boycotting South African firms and products and it became clear that South Africa's domestic market couldn't sustain itself in isolation, the dismantling of apartheid became the only logical option. This doesn't mean, however, that South Africa's last apartheid leaders shouldn't be commended: not all rulers adopt a solution simply because it's logical.

Anything that advances the principle of the oneness of humanity, empowers ever greater numbers of people and impels them to work together for the betterment of their community is, by definition, conducive to development. Working to end ethnic conflict is a community development project. Promoting the advancement of women is a community development project. These actions raise standards of living and save lives.

When people work together, problems are easier to resolve. As 'Abdu'l-Bahá has explained, even if a decision is incorrect, if it is carried out in unity, people will be able to see that it's incorrect and find a better solution more quickly: 'as it is in unity the truth will be revealed and the wrong made right'.[50] The promotion of fellowship and unity also has another benefit: it helps people to approach problems logically and, as a result, makes it more likely that they'll be able to find practicable solutions.

Prejudice, which mars so many human interactions and has led to so much injustice, is a judgement made before the facts are known – or, worse, in disregard of facts that are already available. Prejudice and logic are naturally opposed. This seems to be one of the reasons why Bahá'u'lláh links the establishment of justice with people's willingness to think and investigate problems for themselves:

The best beloved of all things in My sight is Justice; turn not away therefrom if thou desirest Me, and neglect it not that I may confide in thee. By its aid thou shalt see with thine own eyes and not through the eyes of others, and shalt know of thine own knowledge and not through the knowledge of thy neighbour.[51]

Bahá'í consultation is a type of dialogue that is animated by love and which accords everyone a voice – rich or poor, young or old, male or female, native or foreign-born. It is a vehicle, in other words, for problem-solving using the principles of 'fellowship, kindliness and unity'. One of the reasons it works so well is that it's conducive to logical thinking. One of the most egregious logical fallacies is the *ad hominem* argument, which is an irrelevant attack on one's opponent rather than a refutation of his or her ideas. *Ad hominem* arguments are symptomatic of a lack of fellowship. A similar logical fallacy is an appeal to the idea that two wrongs make a right, which one logic textbook defines as 'Defending a wrong by pointing out that our attackers have acted in the same (or an equally bad) manner'.[52] Again, this is a logical fallacy that impedes cooperative undertakings and can be corrected by building bonds of fellowship.

It's hard to argue with 'fellowship' as an idea. We all know that communities function better when people are nice to each other. The problem – and the reason why it's worth exploring this principle and its relationship to positive social action in more depth – is that fellowship can either seem so nebulous or so obvious a concept, depending on one's perspective, that it's easy to read about it without really thinking about it. Fortunately, Bahá'u'lláh gave some specific guidance about what fellowship means and how it can be achieved. For instance: 'Consort with the followers of all religions in a spirit of friendliness and fellowship.'[53] When we consider how disruptive religious conflict is to social and economic development, it's easy to understand how important fellowship is and what an important development project it would be, for example, to help people recognize shared values across their religious beliefs.

At the Rabbani Bahá'í School in India, where between 60 and 80 per cent of the students are Bahá'ís, I asked several Sikhs and

Hindus what it was like to go to a Bahá'í school. They said that they attend Unity Feasts (19 Day Feast-like gatherings that can be attended by those who are not Bahá'ís because community issues aren't discussed) and learn about Bahá'í principles with the rest of the students but they still identify with their own religions and the other students never make fun of them for it; in fact, they didn't seem to think it was an issue.

This might seem like a small thing but not long before I made my visit, Hindus and Muslims had been engaged in retributive massacres across the country. During the worst of the conflict, I was told, people of different religions from the villages around Rabbani had gathered on the school grounds because they believed that at the Bahá'í school, where fellowship among people of different religions is encouraged, they were more likely to be safe.

When the principle of fellowship is applied to governance, one of its most notable manifestations is a rejection of partisanship. Unfortunately, partisan politics is so deeply ingrained in cultures all over the world that it's usually considered perfectly natural. Belize is a case in point. In this small, developing country where partisan politics often seems to prominent, intelligent and fair-minded people to be the most efficient way to tackle the problems they see all around them, one of the results of this philosophy is half-finished houses scattered across the countryside. Before elections, political parties will often promise to build houses for people in exchange for votes. After the elections, if the sponsoring party wins, construction on the houses often stops because the votes are no longer needed. Construction also frequently stops if the other party wins because the new leaders want to punish the losing party's supporters.

This phenomenon isn't limited to small, developing countries; it's just easier to see there. In the United States, it has been suggested that one reason why the US Food and Drug Administration has approved drugs which its own medical officers consider to be ineffective and risky – one drug which has been linked to 49 deaths was approved by the FDA after its advisory committee voted 5–4 that its risks outweighed its benefits – might be the hundreds of millions of dollars that drug companies provide to political campaigns.[54] Across the world in Iraq, meanwhile, about two weeks prior to that country's scheduled elections on 30 January 2005, the Associated Press reported on the deaths of three political candidates with the explanation: 'Sunni Muslim militants, who make up the bulk of Iraq's insurgency, are increasingly honing in on Shiites in their effort to ruin the election that is widely expected to propel their religious rivals to a position of dominance.'[55]

One of the reasons for the success of the American experiment might very well be its founders' attempts to mitigate the effects of partisanship. According to James Madison, the Constitution's chief author and the United States's fourth president, partisan factions were destructive, but inevitable, a fact which the checks and balances of the American political system were designed to address:

> Among the numerous advantages promised by a well-constructed Union, none deserves to be more accurately developed than its tendency to break and control the violence of faction . . . By a faction I understand a number of citizens, whether amounting to a majority or minority of the whole, who are united and actuated by some common impulse of passion, or of interest, adverse to the rights of other citizens, or to the permanent and aggregate interests of the community . . . The inference to which we are brought is that the *causes* of faction cannot be removed and that relief is only to be sought in the means of controlling its *effects*.[56]

George Washington worried that partisanship and factionalism would become institutionalized in the United States through the development of political parties. He explained his concern about political parties in his Farewell Address from the presidency in 1796:

> The alternate domination of one faction over another, sharpened by the spirit of revenge, natural to party dissension, which in different ages and countries has perpetrated the most horrid enormities, is itself a frightful despotism. But this leads at length

to a more formal and permanent despotism. The disorders and miseries, which result, gradually incline the minds of men to seek security and repose in the absolute power of an individual; and sooner or later the chief of some prevailing faction, more able or more fortunate than his competitors, turns this disposition to the purposes of his own elevation, on the ruins of Public Liberty . . . Without looking forward to an extremity of this kind (which nevertheless ought not to be entirely out of sight), the common and continual mischiefs of the spirit of party are sufficient to make it the interest and duty of a wise people to discourage and restrain it.

Today, political parties and representative government are widely imagined to be inextricably linked. Partisanship is taught alongside democracy. Not only do many of the organizations that train people to use democratic systems believe that political parties are inevitable, they also believe that they're beneficial because they theoretically make sure that every group of people is represented – by, of course, defining a 'group of people' in as narrow a way as possible. Since this is the established model, it's one that community developers will have to work with. But the extent to which they can help these different parties of people recognize common goals and build bonds of fellowship is the extent to which their projects will find success.

It's easy to recognize that there's injustice in the world. It's understandable that people will want to protest against it and fight it. But the difference between a development project and a protest movement is that the development project is working towards something, not against something. It has a vision. Groups that are defined by opposition rather than construction are incapable of resolving their communities' problems.

Partisanship is often expressed along ethnic and religious divisions, and this fact has immediate and negative implications for community development. One of the most telling examples of this is the spread of polio. Polio is a disease that, by the time of this writing, should be all but a memory. In the 1980s, 350,000 children were getting polio annually but by 2003 the number of polio cases in the entire world had dropped to 800. This massive reduction was due to the fact that saving someone from the disease is as simple as giving them immunization in the form of mouth drops when he or she is a toddler. Not only is immunization simple and painless, it's free to the people who need it: in Nigeria, one of the disease's last holdouts, the World Health Organization was sending community health workers door to door to give the drops away. A community development project rarely gets much more straightforward than that: giving away something which will potentially make the difference between a life of begging and an active life of productivity.

Unfortunately, many villagers began boycotting the immunizations and three northern Nigerian states eventually banned them. Why? Religious groups claimed that the immunizations were a trick by western governments to spread AIDS and infertility. Some observers have speculated that these Muslim groups were making this claim because of growing tensions between Islam and the United States; others point to campaign tactics by politicians who wanted to discredit the president so that they could win elections. In any case, polio has now spread from Nigeria back into seven nearby countries which had previously eradicated the disease: Ghana, Togo, Benin, Burkina Faso, Central African Republic, Chad and Cameroon.[57] There can hardly be a better example of the fact that until individuals begin to see themselves as a common people, and are able to play a role in their own development, it will take more than good ideas, good technology and sincere intentions to solve their communities' underlying problems.

Vasu Mohan manages democracy and governance projects in Afghanistan, Pakistan, East Timor and India. In his experience, community development projects that don't address ethnic or religious conflicts can't be effective. But this, he acknowledges, is difficult. 'Lots of strategies have been tried,' he says, 'from talks to peace camps. Many projects advance the idea that different groups can learn how to coexist, or that they're separate but equal. These might seem like good ideas in the short term but they backfire in the long run.' The effective community development projects 'are the ones that promote an understanding of the oneness of humanity as clearly as possible. You'd be surprised by how many projects don't do that.'[58]

In the wake of the humanitarian disaster precipitated by the Indian Ocean tsunami at the end of 2004, aid was hampered in some places by the same destructive prejudices that have held people back for generations. In India's Nagapattinam district, where over 6,000 people were killed in the tsunami, Dalits, or untouchables, claimed that they were prevented from receiving aid because of their low caste. One Dalit man who had lost his home said: 'The higher caste fishing community did not allow us to sleep in a marriage hall where they are put up because we belong to the lowest caste.'[59]

Fortunately, many people are quick to recognize that fellowship is the best way to solve their mutual problems, even if it takes a disaster to bring about this realization. After the Indian Ocean tsunami, some government soldiers and low-level officials of the Tamil Tiger rebel forces in Sri Lanka began working together. They cooperated to repair tsunami-damaged roads, while checkpoint commanders on both sides relaxed restrictions to allow for the movement of aid and a government hospital admitted an injured rebel for treatment.[60] On a larger scale, representatives of 150 nations met in Kobe, Japan, at the World Conference on Disaster Reduction from 18 to 22 January 2005 and discussed ways to collaborate to protect people during future disasters. (The conference was scheduled before the Indian Ocean tsunami struck.)[61] As one official pointed out, methods for predicting tsunamis and other natural events exist but they have not been set up in the poor countries which often suffer from them the most.[62] This is something that many countries, both in the afflicted areas and in the rest of the world, were determined to change. During the conference, on 19 January 2005, a United Nations agency announced: 'United Nations experts have decided to create a global early warning system to reduce the impact of natural hazards on vulnerable communities and to increase international cooperation to help save lives and livelihoods.'[63]

Successful community development projects bring people

together. They 'are the ones that allow people to see their true nature and how they are more connected than not,' Mohan explains. 'This is the common element of strategies that work.'[64]

The Material Support of Children's Education

Children, of course, are a community's greatest treasures. They quite literally represent its future and have important roles to play in its present. In the Bahá'í view, children are not merely blank slates. Bahá'u'lláh writes: 'Regard man as a mine rich in gems of inestimable value. Education can, alone, cause it to reveal its treasures, and enable mankind to benefit therefrom.'[65] Unfortunately, for many children, education is a luxury: according to statistics compiled by UNICEF, 246 million children are engaged in 'exploitative labour', 5.6 million of them in 'horrific circumstances' that include bonded labour. A significant number of the children in the latter category (the UNICEF website estimates one million) work in the sex industry. Three hundred thousand children, some as young as eight years old, are exploited as soldiers in armed conflicts.[66]

The Mona Foundation is a non-profit charitable organization dedicated to supporting grassroots educational initiatives and raising the status of women and girls. The Foundation has six criteria for the projects it supports. They need to be founded and operated by local residents. They should have an historic, long-term record of success. They should strive to develop human resources. Their administrators should be active participants in developing plans for their project's self-sustainability.

Two of the criteria specifically relate to how the projects address the needs of children. The programmes should correct 'a vital and significant deficit in the basic needs of children, needs which prevent the full development of their capacity as productive members of their society. These needs must include education, but also may include housing, food and a nurturing environment.' And they should serve children of all backgrounds.[67]

Dr Sohayl Mohajer is the principal of India's Rabbani Bahá'í School, an institution renowned for its community development initiatives. When I asked him what he considered to be the key to successful development, he said, 'After working in community development I'm certain the important thing is educating the children. Teaching the adults is like banging your head against the wall. They say, "I've been illiterate for 40 years and my grandparents were illiterate. Why should I learn to read now?" But if you train the children, in 20 years you have a new society.'[68]

The education of children is also one of the priorities of the global Bahá'í community: not only is universal education a Bahá'í principle but one of the community's current 'core activities' is the grassroots proliferation of classes to teach spiritual principles to children and the training of a vast number of human resources with the capacity to serve as educators.

'Abdu'l-Bahá describes a lack of education as one of the primary impediments to progress. When people become educated, they acquire the skills to express their needs and see that they're met:

> Close investigation will show that the primary cause of oppression and injustice, of unrighteousness, irregularity and disorder, is the people's lack of religious faith and the fact that they are uneducated. When, for example, the people are genuinely religious and are literate and well-schooled, and a difficulty presents itself, they can apply to the local authorities; if they do not meet with justice and secure their rights and if they see that the conduct of the local government is incompatible with the Divine good pleasure and the king's justice, they can then take their case to higher courts and describe the deviation of the local administration from the spiritual law. Those courts can then send for the local records of the case and in this way justice will be done. At present, however, because of their inadequate schooling, most of the population lack even the vocabulary to explain what they want.[69]

'Abdu'l-Bahá also states plainly that education is crucial to empowerment: 'there must be an equality of rights between men and women. Women shall receive an equal privilege of education. This will enable them to qualify and progress in all degrees of occupation and accomplishment.'[70]

The Bahá'í Faith, and therefore Bahá'í development projects, prioritizes the education of women, partly because it is through their education that knowledge can be most effectively diffused throughout a society: 'Furthermore, the education of women is of greater importance than the education of men, for they are the mothers of the race, and mothers rear the children. The first teachers of children are the mothers.'[71]

Save the Children's annual *Mother's Index* shows a direct correlation between the well-being of mothers and of their children. Save the Children identifies six indicators of the well-being of women: lifetime risk of maternal mortality, percentage of women using modern contraception, percentage of births attended by trained personnel, percentage of pregnant women with anaemia, adult female literacy rate and participation of women in the national government. The indicators for children's well-being are identified as infant mortality rate, gross primary enrolment ratio, percentage of population with access to safe water and percentage of children under age five suffering from moderate or severe nutritional wasting. In 2003, out of 117 countries in the index, the same country that ranked first in women's well-being, Sweden, also ranked first in children's well-being. The country which ranked last in women's well-being, Niger, also ranked last in children's well-being.[72]

Geeta Gandhi Kingdon, a Research Officer at the Department of Economics, University of Oxford, pointed out in her essay 'Women, Education and Development', that the 'Education of women improves child health because of the educated mother's greater knowledge of the importance of hygiene and of simple remedies.'

> All of this lowers infant mortality, which in turn means that a family does not need to have a large number of children in order to hedge against the possibility of the premature death of some children. Further, it appears that education of females increases the age at marriage (or cohabitation) and through this delay, lowers

the total fertility rate . . . Finally, some studies find that mother's education has a greater impact on the educational attainment and school achievement of children than father's education.[73]

The tsunami of 26 December 2004 was a natural disaster, the result of a 9.0 magnitude earthquake which there was no way of preventing. The magnitude of the human suffering was incomprehensible. Yet even during this event, a tragedy on a vast scale that was caused by natural phenomena, a significant difference was made in numerous lives because one ten-year-old British school-girl, who happened to be on the island of Phuket in Thailand when the tsunami struck, had received a science education.

'Last term Mr Kearney taught us about earthquakes and how they can cause tsunamis,' the girl informed *The Sun*, a British tabloid. She explained, 'I was on the beach and the water started to go funny. There were bubbles and the tide went out all of a sudden . . . I recognized what was happening and had a feeling there was going to be a tsunami. I told mummy.' Her warning led to the evacuation of Maikhao beach and an adjacent hotel, and was credited with saving hundreds of people from death and injury.[74]

In the early 20th century periodical *Star of the West*, 'Abdu'l-Bahá listed the three cardinal principles that should guide Bahá'í schools, which are paraphrased here:[75]

1) Sincere dedication to the education of children: whole-hearted service to the cause of education, the unfolding of the mysteries of nature, the extension of the boundaries of science, the elimination of the causes of ignorance and social evils, a standard system of instruction, and the diffusion of the lights of knowledge and reality.

2) Moral education: service to the cause of morality, raising the moral tone of the students, inspiring them with the most sublime ethical ideals, teaching them altruism, inculcating in their lives the beauty of holiness and the excellence of virtue, and animating them with the graces and perfections of the religion of God.

33

3) The importance of service: service to humanity and recognition of the oneness of humankind, so that each student may consciously realize that he is a brother to all mankind, irrespective of religion or race. The thoughts of universal peace must be instilled in the minds of all scholars, in order that they may become armies of peace, the real servants of the body politic – the world.

Dr Stephen Waite, the co-founder with his wife, Anne, of Rabbani Bahá'í School in India and the first Dean of Staff and Curriculum Development and then the Vice Principal of Canada's Maxwell International Bahá'í School, explains that because of a Bahá'í school's focus on service, a whole new reciprocal, responsive relationship can develop between the school and the community. The community expresses its needs, which the school tries to fulfil.

Service does not just mean doing things for people, Dr Waite emphasizes. It also involves empowering people to use their own resources to do things for themselves. Schools have an important part to play in this process because education is usually the key to helping communities define and solve their own problems.[76]

You might interpret the principles that were listed at the beginning of this chapter in a much different way than I have. Your assessment of the challenges facing the world and the approaches you want to explore to help resolve them might not have been mentioned here. What matters is that in looking at the world around you, you've seen problems but you're also looking for solutions. So now what? How can we, as individuals, begin to make a difference?

2

Taking Action

A Willingness to Learn

Successful initiatives emerge from a combination of action and reflection. One example is Building Green Bridges, a non-profit organization in Illinois co-founded by Christiana Lawson. In the spring of 2001 Lawson began talking with Chinese friends about community development, education and the need to manage businesses and the environment with virtues-based principles. Lawson's friends weren't sure how all of this could be accomplished. After all, they said, China's leaders were focused on raising capital investment for businesses. They weren't interested in environmental, social or sustainable development. But, says Lawson, 'I was.'

Lawson had devoted a great deal of time to thinking about development. In 1993 and 1994, after becoming curious about how other Bahá'ís were applying Bahá'u'lláh's principles to real-world problems, particularly in the field of health, she gave service to Hospital Bayan in Honduras. From 1994 to 1996 she served at the School of the Nations in Macau, now a Special Administrative Region in China. At the School of the Nations she learned about the Badí' Foundation's projects to empower Chinese women to develop and manage businesses that were sustainable to them, their families, their economy and their environment. She went on to earn a Master's degree in environmental management and in 1999 began working at the US Environmental Protection Agency in Chicago, Illinois.

In the summer of 2001, seeing a need, Lawson started considering ways to promote sustainable development in China. 'Building Green Bridges got its name here,' she says, 'to connect local and national leaders of all countries with best practices to achieve the balance of social concerns': the environment, the society and the economy. 'Some call it the three legs of the stool – or the triple bottom line.'

Lawson had identified a need that was compatible with her interests and skills. She then engaged in two crucial and related activities: she took action and she extended her education in the field.

'In the summer of 2001 I started sharing these ideas with a friend who worked with me at the Federal EPA in Chicago, Krista Durlas,' she explains, 'and I told her I was going to go to China on a two-week trip at the end of October and the beginning of November. I was going to give presentations and share ideas with all the Chinese leaders that my Chinese friends could introduce me to. Krista said she would help, and she did – by the time I was ready to go we had a brochure and business cards. She was coming with me and we would be travelling some of the time with an employee of the Rocky Mountain Institute who would be promoting the hydrogen fuel cell car they'd been developing.'

Building Green Bridges started with that trip. 'We met with hundreds of local leaders and future leaders (college students at several universities) in the Beijing area and Shenyang (a sister city to Chicago in the northeast part of China).'[1] Today, Building Green Bridges links international leaders with practical and meaningful strategies for sustainable development.

What Lawson understood was that a reciprocal relationship exists between learning and action. The people who are the most effective agents of change are those who are constantly trying to educate themselves. When taking action, they do not rely on their assumptions or claim that past successes absolve them of the need to continue exploring and ask questions. They study daily, they investigate the field they are interested in, they evince humility and they practise Bahá'u'lláh's injunction to 'Bring thyself to account each day'.[2]

At the same time, these agents of change take action. They see a need and respond to it. They do not wait until they feel that they are experts. They recognize that much of their expertise will come from hands-on experience and that part of their education comes from their service. Learning, therefore, becomes an ongoing process and a way of life and not a single event to be accomplished and then abandoned.

Leading by Example

When Dr Stephen Waite is asked about what works in the field of education, he says that needs are determined by context. 'What makes something work in, for example, India, or the challenges you face in India, are not the same challenges you have in North America. What I see operating as a universal constant is that schools and education are a human undertaking: anywhere you have dedicated and loving and skilled human beings, you have a circumstance where kids can learn.' Dr Waite goes on to say that his most profound realization about education was that even the most elaborate plans for curriculum and activities do not define a school: people do.[3]

In a discussion at Rabbani on education and development, Dr Sohayl Mohajer explained that the teacher's own rectitude of conduct is part of the training. Deeds are a more powerful teacher than words.[4]

Bahá'í Youth Workshops are youth groups that use performance arts to demonstrate Bahá'í principles. They've been an effective means of sharing these principles in the United States and Canada and have been adopted in many other parts of the world. One reason for their success is the power of art; another is the force of personal example.

Esther Srouji, a member of the Albuquerque Bahá'í Youth Workshop, explained, 'People from outside do see this commitment and intensity. They do see this love and this joy which we have when we're around each other.'[5]

According to an account that I presume is fictional, a woman once brought her son to Mahatma Gandhi and asked Gandhi to convince the boy to stop eating sugar. 'He admires you very much,' the woman said. 'I know he'll stop eating it if you tell him to.'

'Bring him back in a month,' Gandhi said.

The woman agreed. The next month, as promised, she brought her son to Gandhi.

'You should stop eating sugar,' Gandhi said to the boy. The boy, impressed with anything Gandhi had to say, readily agreed.

'If that's all you were going to say, why couldn't you have said it a month ago?' the woman asked Gandhi.

'Because', said Gandhi, 'last month I was eating sugar.'

The first task of anyone who wishes to teach others is to teach him or herself. 'Whoso ariseth among you to teach the Cause of his Lord,' Bahá'u'lláh counsels, 'let him, before all else, teach his own self, that his speech may attract the hearts of them that hear him.'[6]

Communication

How we communicate with others obviously plays a role in how our message is accepted. Bahá'u'lláh provides guidance about how we should share information with others:

> Show forbearance and benevolence and love to one another. Should any one among you be incapable of grasping a certain truth, or be striving to comprehend it, show forth, when conversing with him, a spirit of extreme kindliness and good-will. Help him to see and recognize the truth, without esteeming yourself to be, in the least, superior to him, or to be possessed of greater endowments.[7]

When development experts come from outside to help local people raise their standard of living, it's distressingly easy for them to start treating the locals as inferiors. Needless to say, this approach isn't particularly effective. People respond best to respect and it's easy for most people to tell whether the person who is speaking to them respects them or not.

Our ability to communicate effectively, Bahá'u'lláh tells us, is linked to our own self-development: 'Unless he teacheth his own self, the words of his mouth will not influence the heart of the seeker.'[8]

One example of effective multicultural communication comes from the Women's Mid-Decade Dialogue in 1983, which was sponsored by the Young Women's Christian Association. Mildred Persinger, chair of the World Issues Sub-committee of the YWCA's National Board, explained in the project report that 'the message of the Women's Mid-Decade Dialogue is that seemingly over-whelmingly international issues can be translated to human scale through personal interaction and dialogue. The programme aimed to stimulate interest in local/global connection by involving US committees in dialogue around shared concerns with women from eight countries of Asia, Africa, Latin America and the Pacific.'

According to Roshan R. Billimoria, the programme coordi-nator for the YWCA, the Dialogue ran into problems in certain areas, such as Atlanta, where the local coordinators and interna-tional partners had different expectations. However, there were also many success stories, such as in South Carolina:

> Team I arrived in Hemingway, South Carolina to quite a change of pace and locale. Here was a 'developing' community – rural, largely poor, largely black; in tobacco growing country; struggling directly with the self-same concerns of health, education and employment so vital a part of the development dialogue in coun-tries of the third world. The Hemingway partners were educated but not necessarily schooled; they were global in outlook but had in most instances not travelled too far from their own homes and neighbourhoods. The quality of the exchanges reflected rooted-ness in the deep reds and browns of the soil.
>
> The Hemingway Dialogue was hosted jointly by the Louis Gregory Bahá'í Institute and the Florence Chapters of the National Council of Negro Women [and conducted] at the Gregory Institute itself and in the surrounding homes and churches.

The dialogue participants obviously respected each other; perhaps it helped that even though they came from different places, they were able to recognize their common connections, since all had the 'self-same concerns'. The local coordinators and international participants consulted with Hemingway residents at private homes, churches and schools throughout the area. In the words of Billimoria, 'There was no doubt of the impact of the programme on those who were involved in it. The local coordinators spoke of the value of such a programme in 'improving community relations'; in underscoring the mutual support and solidarity that flowed between the residents of this small rural American community and the learning partners from afar . . .'[9]

Personal Conduct

We can't work for the world if we neglect our immediate surroundings. As the popular expression goes, 'Think globally, act locally'. We have expanding circles of responsibility, which begin with our own personal relationship with God, expand to our responsibilities to our family and the people around us and eventually reach out to include the whole world. These concentric circles are all important but each one depends to some extent on the one within it.

The foundation of civilization is love. Love on a societal level is manifested as justice and love on an individual level is expressed through compassion and mercy.[10] Love and kindness are the indispensable traits of anyone who wants to build a better world. In the words of Bahá'u'lláh:

> Be a treasure to the poor, an admonisher to the rich, an answerer of the cry of the needy, a preserver of the sanctity of thy pledge. Be fair in thy judgement, and guarded in thy speech. Be unjust to no man, and show all meekness to all men.[11]

To Gandhi, how people approached a goal was at least as important as the achievement of the goal itself:

They say 'means are after all means'. I would say 'means are after all everything'. As the means so the end. There is no wall of separation between means and end. Indeed the Creator has given us control (and that too very limited) over means, none over end. Realization of the goal is in exact proportion to that of the means. This is a proposition that admits no exception.[12]

Mahatma Gandhi's goal, which he and his countrymen successfully realized, was to win independence from the world's most powerful empire without shedding blood.

If we violate our principles, we subvert the very purpose of our actions. This is true even when the violations seem immediately pragmatic. For example, after the US invaded Afghanistan in 2001, the international community sent a representative to help the country establish a new government. The Afghans knew what kind of government they wanted and what kind of people they wanted to be in it. What they didn't want was anyone who had violated human rights, and in particular the local warlords, to be put into positions of power. But the international representative overrode their concerns and made the warlords prominent members of the new power structure because they were already in control of fighters and guns.[13] No one who supported this decision thought that the warlords were ideal leaders; what they thought was that it was easier in the short run to let them keep their power and their guns, and the end justified the means.

This was a perfectly practical decision. Unfortunately, it contributed to more national instability. In July 2004, Médecins Sans Frontières, a prominent human rights agency, announced that it was leaving Afghanistan because of deteriorating security conditions. They had been operating in the country for 24 years.[14] Something is definitely wrong when an organization that has stayed in a country through 17 years of war suddenly decides that the situation has become too dangerous to remain.

Being principled doesn't mean being dogmatic or impractical. It simply means remembering our ultimate objectives and not abandoning them for the sake of expediency. It means keeping in mind the reason we're doing what we're doing and trying to align our actions with our words.

The importance of remaining true to principle is discussed in *Century of Light*, a 2001 document prepared under the supervision of the Universal House of Justice:

> Because [the Bahá'í International Community, the agency that represents the Bahá'ís to international organizations] is, and is seen to be, entirely non-partisan, it has increasingly been trusted as a mediating voice in complex, and often stressful, discussions in international circles on major issues of social progress. This reputation has been strengthened by appreciation of the fact that the Community refrains, on principle, from taking advantage of such trust to press partisan agendas of its own. By 1968, a Bahá'í representative had been elected to membership on the Executive Committee of Non-Governmental Organizations [affiliated with the Office of Public Information of the United Nations], subsequently holding the positions of chairman and vice-chairman. From this point on, representatives of the Community found themselves increasingly asked to function as convenors or chairpersons of a wide range of bodies . . .[15]

If we say that the end justifies the means, how do we know when we've reached the end? New conditions face us every day. We are contributing to the shape of our world on a continuous basis by the processes we engage in and the structures we build to sustain them. So, as *Century of Light* points out, 'The structure of the Bahá'í International Community reflects the principles guiding its work.'[16]

The challenges we face in our own work will usually be less extreme than those faced by colonial Indians, millennial Afghans or the Bahá'í International Community in the 20th century but we can safely count on being challenged. We can also be confident that successfully dealing with these challenges will require constant self-development.

Our development needs to be constant because we're never

standing in place, whether we think we are or not. Everything in this world is constantly changing, and anything that does not progress is regressing. 'Absolute repose does not exist in nature,' 'Abdu'l-Bahá explains. 'All things either make progress or lose ground. Everything moves forward or backward, nothing is without motion.'[17]

Our human progress, 'Abdu'l-Bahá says, is the result of spirit being expressed in the material world; this is the source of our achievement.

> In the world of spirit there is no retrogression. The world of mortality is a world of contradictions, of opposites; motion being compulsory everything must either go forward or retreat. In the realm of spirit there is no retreat possible, all movement is bound to be towards a perfect state. 'Progress' is the expression of spirit in the world of matter. The intelligence of man, his reasoning powers, his knowledge, his scientific achievements, all these being manifestations of the spirit, partake of the inevitable law of spiritual progress and are, therefore, of necessity, immortal.[18]

Spiritual virtues are essential tools for anyone hoping to effect positive social change. Honesty is a prerequisite for both individual development and collective progress. Without honesty, our progress can't even be evaluated.

Patience is another requirement for most community development work. Many people labour for years at important tasks without ever receiving recognition. When large victories are advertised, they're often the result of long hours and many smaller efforts. It is through our continual commitment to our ideals that our capacities increase and advances are gained. Lasting accomplishments are the result of everyday tasks and the way people live their lives. It sometimes helps to be in the right place at the right time but even the right place can't help us if we haven't worked to make ourselves ready to take advantage of our opportunities.

The teachings of the Buddha, the Bible, the Qur'án, and the Bahá'í writings have all explained how we can improve our personal lives and all indicate that there is a correlation between personal conduct and the success of social action.

There are a few practices that seem to help people in their personal development. Saying prayers and reading sacred scriptures every day connect us to a higher source of power, give us guidance and expand our vision. Translating our vision into acts of service provides meaning to our lives. Without action all we have are words. Through action we gain strength and spiritual confirmation; with our vision of permanent ideals, transitory setbacks cease to deter us.

'The Keynote of success in the teaching field is study of the Word, Prayer, Meditation; and then action,' Shoghi Effendi explains through his secretary. 'Above all, perseverance in action. When these steps are followed in the realm of self-sacrifice, success will be achieved.'[19]

Exercising, eating well and getting enough rest clarify our minds and improve our moods. Setting ourselves personal goals and engaging in reflection and self-evaluation each day help us to assess our progress. Looking at our lives to see what brings us happiness and what brings us down, and working to sustain those things that bring us happiness, lift our spirits and energies.

Self-awareness is crucial to personal development. Cultivation of the knowledge of God and of ourselves is a reciprocal process. Bahá'u'lláh tells us, 'Thy spirit is My place of revelation'[20] and 'Turn thy sight unto thyself, that thou mayest find Me standing within thee, mighty, powerful and self-subsisting.'[21]

None of this is easy. And, of course, we don't have to wait until we're perfect before our actions start making an impact on the rest of the world; our actions make an impact today. What's striking, then, is not that people make mistakes or that political, business and spiritual leaders seem to be in the habit these days of resigning from their posts in disgrace. What's striking and worth considering, for anyone who is intentionally trying to influence society, is how before being publicly exposed these leaders continue to cause damage while thinking, or at least pretending to think, that everything they're doing is right.

People rarely decide to be villains. Many people manage to convince themselves that they're doing well while accomplishing great harm. To cite an extreme example, Adolf Hitler never got up in the morning and said, 'I'm going to do all the wrong things today.' What he actually wrote, in *Mein Kampf*, was 'I am convinced that I am acting as the agent of our Creator.'[22] This isn't just a failing of dictators; economists have found that professionals often think they know much more than they actually do. As the writer James Surowiecki put it, 'it wasn't just that they were wrong; they also didn't have any idea how wrong they were.'[23]

We cannot always control the ultimate outcomes of our actions but we can try to control our level of sincerity. We can also protect ourselves by calling ourselves to account each day: measuring our actions against our goals and trying to determine the real impact we're having. This becomes easier when we've set standards for ourselves. For many people, these standards are found in holy scriptures. At the very least, they should be based on honest reflection. Self-evaluation is only possible if we're open to questioning ourselves.

When one looks back at the parade of failed leaders who have hacked, slaved and burned their way through history, it's hard to reconcile their actions with their often firm convictions that they were on the side of light and holiness and everything else that was good. This contradiction begins to make sense when one realizes that many of these people did display moral behaviours; they were just selective about the groups to which they chose to reveal this side of themselves. There were generous slave owners, for example, and there were people who kept their wives and concubines locked away in harems but were quite solicitous of the views of other men. Hitler might really have thought that he was helping the Germans, as long as Jews, Roma and many other groups were not counted as Germans. In this context, it becomes easy to see that by expanding our vision of community to include all peoples, Bahá'u'lláh has redefined what it means to be a moral person and made it harder for people to cause harm in the name of good. If you want to make sure that you're helping the world and not hurting it, build unity and eradicate prejudice.

Another impediment to realizing good intentions is every person's individual nemesis: his or her own ego. One of the symptoms of insecurity is self-centredness and its effects on organizations and projects can be debilitating. Wounded pride compels people to derail their projects for the sake of vindictiveness. Self-doubt motivates people to seize opportunities for immediate fame or advancement at the expense of long-term goals. In 378, at the battle of Hadrianople, the Roman Emperor Valens engaged the Goths before his nephew Gratian arrived with reinforcements because he was jealous of the young man's military reputation. The result was the devastation of his legions, his own death and what the historian J. B. Bury has called 'one of the landmarks of history – one of the three most famous disasters that befell Rome in her conflict with the Germans.'[24]

Although questions of ego ultimately require soul-searching on the part of individuals, some organizations explicitly attempt to avoid building cults of personality. For example, while it's always a good idea to recognize the people who have worked hard on an organization's behalf, many organizations try to keep mention of board members to a minimum in their publications.

'We behold it [the world], in this day, at the mercy of rulers so drunk with pride that they cannot discern clearly their own best advantage, much less recognize a Revelation so bewildering and challenging as this,' Bahá'u'lláh declares. 'And whenever any one of them hath striven to improve its condition, his motive hath been his own gain, whether confessedly so or not; and the unworthiness of this motive hath limited his power to heal or cure.'[25]

All of the foregoing should be tempered with a message relayed by the National Spiritual Assembly of the Bahá'ís of the United States to junior Bahá'í youth in 2001: we can make mistakes and still accomplish our spiritual missions.[26]

Mistakes, presuming that we learn from them, can be a positive sign of creativity and exploration. And we could use a lot more of both, because the world needs new solutions, such as the innovative solar cooker that the Barli Development Institute for Rural Women trains villagers to use in India. By taking advantage of sunlight to cook meals, the solar cooker reduces the number of trees being cut down for firewood while saving the women money, time and energy.[27]

We don't end up with inventions like the solar cooker, or the training that the Barli Development Institute provides along with it, by putting a lot of effort into avoiding making errors. We end up with them by increasing our capacity for positive action. One way to increase this capacity is to cultivate a new model of leadership.

Moral Leadership

The problems facing humanity aren't primarily material. They're mental and social.

We currently have more than enough food, for example, to nourish every person on the planet. That's why small armies of children roam the mountainous garbage dumps outside of Tampico, Mexico: there's enough food but that's the most accessible place the social and political system the children live in have placed it.

One of the most telling places to observe the impact of human will on the human condition is in those natural disasters we call 'acts of God'. By November 1998, violent weather had cost the world $89 billion for the year – more than the loss for the entire decade of the 1980s. Storms, floods, droughts and fires in 1998 also killed about 32,000 people and displaced 300 million.

The Worldwatch Institute and the world's largest insurer, Germany's Munich Re, blamed people, often for catalysing climate change and razing forests. 'More and more, there's a human fingerprint in natural disasters in that we're making them more frequent and more intense and . . . more destructive,' said Seth Dunn, one of Worldwatch's climate change experts. 'In a sense, we're turning up the faucets . . . and throwing away the sponges, like the forests and the wetlands.'[28]

A number of mental models have contributed to this phenomenon. One is the fundamental misapprehension that certain communities can ultimately prosper at the expense of the human family as a whole.

In the face of our mounting environmental pressures, it's immediately apparent that current social structures are inadequate to confront the danger. Quite simply, what happens in one country can affect the environment of another, rendering borders irrelevant. It's no surprise, then, that one of the earliest prominent signs of global consultation on a pressing issue was the 1992 'Earth Summit' in Rio de Janeiro, Brazil, where over 150 states signed the United Nations Framework Convention on Climate Change. The text states that the parties to the convention acknowledge 'that change in the Earth's climate and its adverse effects are a common concern of humankind'.

The signatories to such an agreement, however, aren't only thinking about the issue at hand, in this case the environment; they're also thinking, quite rationally, about the demands of the social structures that they're a part of. Although the US ratified the treaty, the Senate passed a resolution 'Expressing the sense of the Senate regarding the conditions for the United States becoming a signatory', which stated that the Senate wanted developing countries to share responsibility with the developed world and that it wanted to make sure that no treaties harmed the economy of the United States.

In short, our social structures reflect our mind sets. You have to believe certain things about human nature to want to live in a democracy as opposed to, say, an autocracy. And our mind sets, our mental models, are influenced by our experiences of interacting with the society we live in.

The reason so many people do so many seemingly inexplicable things is that often they've found them to work in their own lives. Their actions are honed by the negative and positive reinforcement they receive from the daily responses of the people all around them, responses which also help to shape the way they view the world. Many of the issues that we consider to be pressing social problems are rooted in perspectives that make perfect sense to the people who hold them.

In Belize City, young, single, impoverished and undereducated mothers were raising a large number of equally uneducated and impoverished children, who were in turn contributing to a crime epidemic that was prompting travel warnings not only from the US Department of State but from the residents of the country's other towns and villages. The amazing thing about this trend was that it was being sustained on purpose. For young men at that time, the prestige that made a difference in their daily lives wasn't measured merely by how many women they'd had sex with but by how many children they'd fathered, and the ongoing crime spree all around them was one of the results.

Another example is the distrust that several fundamentalist religious groups show towards attempts to work for peace and to foster cooperation between countries, which is based on their belief that the antichrist will take over the world through an international alliance. The same doctrines hold that the world will have to get worse before God descends to judge it, which means that it's pointless, and perhaps even counterproductive (because it will prolong the end times) to try to resolve the world's mounting social crises.[29]

On the other hand, consider the uncountable number of schools, hospitals, orphanages and other charitable institutions that have been raised over the centuries because Christians had an image in their mind of how Jesus treated the poor, and perceived His love in their hearts.

According to Dr Eloy Anello, the president of Bolivia's Núr University, our behaviour is influenced by our mental models of how the world works. It follows, then, that if we're going to change our behaviour we need to change our mental models. And in order to change these models, we have to form an awareness of the models we're using in the first place. This means identifying the beliefs, prejudices and attitudes that contribute to our outlook, a set of concepts that we usually learn from the societies in which we are raised.

Sami, who conducts analysis for the World Bank, points out that our mental models can affect how we look at something even as seemingly simple as poverty. 'One of the greatest challenges in development, in my mind, is that development workers are often not aware of what it means to live in a poor community,' she says.

'. . .What does it mean to be poor? Does it mean not having material wealth? Have you ever thought about why in many languages, we refer to someone that we feel sympathy towards as a "poor" person?' Why don't we feel a corresponding sense of sympathy for very wealthy people who live a life of seclusion because they can't cope with life's realities?

> These questions force us to think about concepts like poverty and inequality. Perhaps we need to reorient ourselves and step out of the materialist box we refer to as 'development'. If we step out of this box, we will realize that no country in the world can call itself 'developed' because we will see 'development' as a stage of human progress that corresponds to the actualization of the oneness of humankind, where no one suffers at the expense of another.[30]

Dr Anello asserts that a new mental model, one of 'moral leadership', is conducive to personal transformation. In the book *Moral Leadership*, he and Joan Barstow Hernández identify six elements that form this model's foundation:

1) Belief in the essential nobility of human nature

Our assumptions about human nature determine how we treat other people. They also influence our expectations of ourselves.

The mental framework of moral leadership is based on the conviction that the human being is essentially noble and that our noble characteristics can be drawn out through education.

2) Service-oriented leadership

Many people equate leadership with domination. Moral leadership is about serving the community and helping others to develop their capacities to serve as well.

True leaders determine what their communities need and work on achieving it, even if other jobs are more glamorous. They've detached themselves from expectations of recognition and reward.

3) The purpose of leadership: personal and social transformation

Central to moral leadership is the concept that human life has a dual purpose: personal and social transformation. Personal transformation means drawing out peoples' latent potentialities; social transformation means promoting an ever-advancing civilization based on justice, unity and love. These goals are mutually reinforcing.

Groups that are interested in social and personal transformation must have a vision of the ideal towards which they are striving. They must also work on the development of the capabilities that lead to these ideals. 'The active effort of the group to serve others,' Anello and Hernández explain, 'by means of teaching what they have learned and by striving to apply the moral leadership capabilities in their personal lives, with their families, in the organizations in which they work, or in the community in general, helps to consolidate the process of personal transformation and to initiate and sustain the process of social transformation.'

4) The moral responsibility of investigating and applying truth

Moral leadership is a discipline that requires active investigation. Its adherents have a responsibility to seek out the truth and to apply it in their own lives so that these lives can become internally and externally consistent and harmonious with the underlying structure of reality.

5) Transcendence

Rather than exercising leadership for one's own benefit, moral leadership calls on individuals to serve the common good, participate in an ongoing learning process, strive for the transformation of society, develop moral self-discipline in their moral lives and continually search after truth. This challenging mandate requires a source of inspiration: a vision of eternal values that transcends more mundane concerns.

6) The development of capabilities

Traditionally, when we've thought of moral people, we've thought of passive followers who wouldn't rock the boat. The contemporary age calls for social actors who are positively engaged in transformation. These actors need to develop the internal capabilities that can allow them to act for the promotion of the common good.[31]

In 1992 a non-profit organization called Health for Humanity began a campaign to improve vision in Albania. The project was developed through extensive consultation with the local Albanian ophthalmic community and among other activities it helped the country develop its capacity to perform modern cataract surgery. In 2002, though, the organization realized that the project now required more than medical technology and education: it also needed moral leadership. One of the problems the project faced was that some doctors, who had learned during the Communist period to wield knowledge as a bargaining tool, refused to give up perceived power by training their residents. Health for Humanity asked Núr University to train the programme participants in moral leadership, and the situation improved.[32]

3

Responding to Needs

Addressing People's Concerns

'These are not days of prosperity and triumph,' Bahá'u'lláh has told us. 'The whole of mankind is in the grip of manifold ills. Strive, therefore, to save its life through the wholesome medicine which the almighty hand of the unerring Physician hath prepared.'[1]

'The Bahá'í Faith has a message for everyone on this planet,' Dr Hidayatu'lláh Ahmadiyeh said in a talk at the July 1988 Bahá'í Youth Conference in Juarez, Mexico. 'Are we looking at that message? In other words, the Bahá'í Faith has medicine for every sickness . . .

> Now, let me give you an example. Imagine that you have a problem with your children and you want someone to guide you on that issue. Instead, somebody comes and tells you about the world government that is going to be established, about the federation of the nations . . . about the world tribunal, all these things which are not relating at all to your *acute* desire to know how you are going to guide your son, who is rebelling, how you are going to show the way to your daughter, who does not look to any authority with confidence, who is confused. But when we are talking to you, we are talking about other things.

'Sometimes we think that we must teach the people whatever we know,' Dr Ahmadiyeh explained. 'But this is wrong, really. We must teach what the people need and what is most important to them.'²

As Dr Moojan Momen has pointed out, this is how 'Abdu'l-Bahá taught His father's Faith to North Americans:

He chose those teachings that addressed the topical issues of the day and were of most concern to the sort of people that he was addressing – issues such as women's rights (this period saw a peak in the activities of the suffragette movement), the harmony of religion and science (this was still a hotly debated issue following the controversies over Darwin's theories), etc.³

As for agriculture, the importance of which Bahá'u'lláh had emphasized, "Abdu'l-Bahá apparently judged that this teaching of Bahá'u'lláh would be of little interest to the predominantly urban audiences whom he addressed".⁴

Every community has specific needs. At his talk at the Sydney Bahá'í Centre in November 2003, Dr Peter Khan noted that

Social and economic development has a particular form in Third World countries where there is endemic poverty; there are great needs for hygiene and health and collective generation of income but we are still working out what to do in developed western society such as this one in the way of social and economic development.⁵

Dr Khan suggested four areas in which Bahá'ís could make contributions to the social and economic development of western countries: working on strengthening marriage; offering positive values for children; offering the wider society a place for safe social interaction where people feel that they can socialize, relax and trust strangers; and offering advice, examples and guidance to people who are searching for meaning in their lives.⁶

The Badí' Foundation is a prime example of an organization that bases its programmes on the needs of the community. Its president, Dr Noguchi, explains how its projects are determined:

The social enterprises are developed by the participants so our role is to help them identify their own capacities and the kind of assistance they might need to make it work, not to evaluate whether it is worth pursuing or not. Where there seems to be a consistent need and interest by many people in a specific area, we may develop additional courses to help groups that want to pursue that type of social enterprise. That is basically how the current social enterprise specializations were developed. However, we have resources, so decisions also need to take into account the availability of resources and the possibilities we see for the impact of the programme.[7]

In a letter written in 1931, Shoghi Effendi referred clearly to the bankruptcy of movements that place their own perpetuation, their leaders' ambitions or any other goals above the needs and conditions of the people whose lives they are created to benefit:

The call of Bahá'u'lláh is primarily directed against all forms of provincialism, all insularities and prejudices. If long-cherished ideals and time-honoured institutions, if certain social assumptions and religious formulae have ceased to promote the welfare of the generality of mankind, if they no longer minister to the needs of a continually evolving humanity, let them be swept away and relegated to the limbo of obsolescent and forgotten doctrines. Why should these, in a world subject to the immutable law of change and decay, be exempt from the deterioration that must needs overtake every human institution? For legal standards, political and economic theories are solely designed to safeguard the interests of humanity as a whole, and not humanity to be crucified for the preservation of the integrity of any particular law or doctrine.[8]

Targeting Core Issues

Brazil is like many places in the world with an entrenched tradition of child labour. There is a long history of opposition to the practice, with laws protecting children going back to 1891. Yet by 2000, according to a *Washington Post* report, 2.5 million children in the country were working.[9]

The Association for the Cohesive Development of the Amazon (ADCAM) tries to make some of these children's lives better. It has agreements with federal, state and city government agencies to provide children with access to extracurricular activities, such as sports, arts, recreation and cultural experiences, after work hours.

However, these activities can't replace school and telling parents that their kids shouldn't work isn't going to solve the problem. So ADCAM also targets some of the reasons that children work in the first place. It helps families to understand the importance of education and it develops income-generating enterprises to reduce their financial reliance on child labour.[10]

Successful projects address the core issues that lie beneath the problems. That's not surprising; it's ultimately more effective to target a cause than a symptom. The question is, how do you make sure that the core issues are being targeted? One way is to help develop projects that are driven from the grassroots rather than from above.

In 2004 I asked Mojgan Sami how to make sure that a project could be sustained. 'First, we have to define what you mean by a "sustainable project", she pointed out. 'Are you defining this in terms of environmental and social sustainability, or whether this project will receive the support it needs from local beneficiaries in order to be successfully implemented and used to benefit the local community? If you are speaking about the first definition, then the standard definition of sustainability is generally agreed as "Meeting the needs of the present generation without compromising the ability of future generations to meet their own needs" (as defined by the Brundtland Commission, 1987). If you are speaking about the latter form of sustainability, then the magic answer is: "Make sure you are implementing a project that has been identified as a high priority by the *beneficiaries* (not by the national government, not by donor agencies, not by you)."'[11]

Professor Hanson notes the same thing in her book *Social and Economic Development*. When projects are developed from the grassroots through the power of consultation, there's a better chance that they'll be projects that the community is willing to support – and is capable of supporting.[12]

Vasu Mohan cites three strategies that can help a project to be sustained. The first is that there should be significant overlap between the people who initiate a project, the people who implement it and the people who benefit from it. The ideal is for these to all be the same people. Such a project, says Mohan, 'is very, very likely to be sustainable' because it leads to a sense of ownership and commitment among all the players.

Second, there should a sense of humility among the key players. 'Experts don't usually ask "What do I have to offer, what can I learn?"' he says, but they should.

Finally, the project should address the roots of the problem. For a programme to last, people have to see results. And this is more likely to happen the more closely it targets the conditions that are contributing to whatever people want to see changed.[13]

To Dr Javid, making decisions at the grassroots is one of the fundamental ways to make sure that the contributing factors of a problem are being addressed.

'I think that the fundamental challenge for westerners is to allow the mind-shift that's required in order to build capacity at the grassroots and human resources in the field,' she says.

> The way you go into a project, consult and interact with the agencies that you're supporting requires a fundamentally different approach to collaboration than what we know of here [in the West]. People I think are beginning to understand that a little bit. [We have to learn] to respect the learning at the grassroots and allow for it. [We should] not impose expertise on them unless asked. [We need to] allow for collaboration with other like-minded organizations and devise parallel lines of action that will in fact impact the core problem.[14]

Grassroots-driven initiatives also have another benefit. The devolution of as much authority as possible to local decision-making bodies is a bulwark against oppression. 'To cast aside centralization which promotes despotism is the exigency of the time,' says 'Abdu'l-Bahá.[15] Centralization has its place: the original 13 American colonies entered a new stage of development when they federated as the United States. But they also added to their collective value by retaining their diversity and local decision-making capacities.

Integration

As discussed above, a successful development project targets core issues. However, anyone who looks for these issues realizes that they don't exist in isolation. 'Our experience is that there's not one cause of a social problem, so it has to be worked at aggregate,' Dr Javid explains.[16]

One example of a development project that addresses core problems by working in aggregate is Hospital Bayan in Honduras. Hospital Bayan has an integrated approach to health. It provides surgeons to people who wouldn't normally have access to them. It also provides medical training to local healers who don't have academic credentials, since those are often the people who will be the first to give a local response. It provides a travelling clinic. It relates health to the environment by showing people how to cope with cholera outbreaks and explaining the dangers of smoke from cooking fires in unventilated houses. Community meetings discuss methods of coping with tourism in ways that can mitigate negative environmental and social impacts to the community. 'So they weren't just targeting symptoms, like stitching machete wounds,' says Christiana Lawson, who participated in some of Hospital Bayan's activities. 'They were addressing the causes, like domestic violence and alcoholism.'[17]

Innovative thinkers are trying to figure out new ways to address the challenge of integration. Arthur Lyon Dahl is a marine biologist who has pioneered a holistic approach to contemporary problems by combining the concept of economics, or how to manage a system, with ecology, how to understand it. He calls this idea the eco principle. His approach is a way of looking at a whole system, man-made or natural, of any scale. An eco is a functional system with distinct features enclosed by clear boundaries. Understanding an eco requires understanding its content or resources, the loss and gain of these resources, the input and output of energy and its change over time. Crucial to any eco's success is its information content, which can also be described as its internal systems and organization, and its communication with other ecos.

By looking at systems from this perspective, Dahl posits, whether a household or a nation or a forest or the planet, one can come to an understanding of its status and what it needs to improve or sustain it, with balance of material inputs and outputs being a primary goal. According to this theory, information and connectivity, not materials, constitute an eco's true wealth.[18]

'The trend towards more comprehensive, integrated approaches to development is present throughout the world and its institutions,' says Sami. No one speaks of 'development' anymore without qualifying it. We often hear references to 'social and economic development' or 'community-based development' or 'rights-based approach to development'. International financial institutions, such as the World Bank, have been increasingly moving from a 'project-oriented' view of development to more programmatic approaches which involve many sectors.

'In fact,' Sami explains, 'studies have shown that multi-sectoral approaches to development enhance development effectiveness and lead to better outcomes than traditional single-sector projects.'

For instance, in a certain country in Africa it was recognized that transportation projects need to include a health component because it was determined that HIV/AIDS is more prevalent on truck routes. By ensuring that the ministries of health and transportation consult with one another to develop more integrated approaches to building roads, this country was empowered to decrease new cases of HIV/AIDS. Although this multi-sectoral approach to development may seem like common sense, the fact is that it is difficult and challenging to bring sectoral specialists together because they often do not speak the same language, although they are seeking the same results. For example, generally speaking, economists speak with 'numbers' and social scientists speak with 'stories'. Bringing different disciplines around a table together to address common concerns (reducing poverty, improving health and education, etc.) is one thing. Ensuring that they understand each other's approaches to find solutions is another. How can we overcome this challenge? My experience has demonstrated that increased dialogue . . . better enables development workers to ensure that development results are more effective.[19]

Collaborations can also build grassroots support. Health for Humanity gains support and knowledge from the community by frequently collaborating with local and like-minded organizations. In order to avoid confusion, the terms and lengths of the collaboration agreements are clearly spelled out at the beginning.

Wally Verderoon, a member of Health for Humanity's board of directors who has helped non-profit organizations of all sizes to raise funds, points out that partnerships can also help organizations receive funding from grant-making foundations. 'Foundations love partnerships,' he says. 'Universities love interdisciplinary projects. They want the biggest bang for the buck. They also want to avoid replication. And partnerships build strength.' He recommends that agreements with partner agencies, and their specific roles, be mentioned in grant proposals. One of the first questions to ask when planning a project should be, 'Is anyone else doing this and can we get them involved?'[20]

4

Community Engagement

The Oneness of Humanity

Over the course of the past three chapters we've been looking at the same theme from different angles. Whether we've been considering a universal auxiliary language, collective action in response to environmental degradation or collaborative approaches to economic development, we've observed that social problems are exacerbated by humanity's artificial divisions and alleviated by actions that recognize our essential unity. The fundamental social principle of the Bahá'í Faith, and therefore the fulcrum of every Bahá'í-inspired effort at social change, is the oneness of humanity.

The earliest Bahá'ís didn't look much different from other Iranians. They didn't have a broad understanding of Bahá'u'lláh's teachings or how they could be applied. That eventually changed, of course, and they became renowned for their generally high level of education and other attainments. According to Dr Moojan Momen, one of the reasons for this change was that 'Abdu'l-Bahá invited Bahá'ís from the United States, most of them women, to live among the Iranian Bahá'ís and engage in projects to advance the Iranians' health and education.

This had an enormous effect on the Bahá'í community in Iran. Apart from the obvious effect of confirming the supranational character of the religion, it gave the Bahá'í women of Iran some idea of what they could achieve as they sought to improve their position in society. Partly as a result of the efforts of these Americans and

partly as a result of the endeavours of the Iranian Bahá'ís themselves, the Iranian Bahá'í community, which had, until that time,
been scarcely any different from the rest of Islamic Iran, began
to put into practice such Bahá'í teachings as the importance of
education and the elevation of the role of women and thus began
to emerge as a progressive and vital force in Iran.[1]

Community development projects often bring in outside experts
to assist a local population. The danger of this approach is that
local people will come to depend on the experts. This is what happened to Bosnia after it was rescued by prosperous agencies from
abroad. As *The Atlantic Monthly* pointed out in 2004, 'the High
Representative acts as a viceroy presiding over a colonial depend-
ency that is without either democracy or self-government. Neither
there nor in Kosovo is an exit strategy evident, because the depar-
ture of the international community would leave both places with
the intractable political problems that led to intervention in the
first place.'[2]

How was this dilemma avoided by the early Bahá'ís? There
are probably several answers; one was identified by Dr Farzam
Arbab in the early 1970s while he was a visiting professor at
the Universidad del Valle in Colombia, helping to reorganize its
department of physics. While there the professor was invited to
participate in an interdisciplinary group that was discussing integrated approaches to rural development. At the same time he and
his wife were interacting with the rural Bahá'í community. The
gap between the group's interesting theories and the challenges
of the real community led Arbab to withdraw gradually from that
group and start, with a group of colleagues, an new organization
called Fundación para la Aplicación y Enseñanza de las Ciencias
(Foundation for the Application and Teaching of the Sciences) or
FUNDAEC.

One of the ideas at the heart of FUNDAEC was that devel-
opmental models of the past, which saw development as an
intervention and involved local people in plans brought in from
abroad – which, in essence, looked at the developers as outsiders

– needed to be changed. It was a model that saw separation as the norm: 'the dividing of people into groups of "we" and "they" who fight, who compete, who negotiate, who cooperate, or help each other from across the boundaries that define their separateness'. FUNDAEC's approach was a complete realignment. 'Viewed from the angle of oneness, development ceases to be something one does for others. A vision begins to emerge according to which the rich and the poor, the illiterate, the educated, are all to participate in building a new civilization . . .'[3]

Perhaps this is one of the reasons why 'Abdu'l-Bahá's approach to development was so successful. He didn't ask American Bahá'ís to help Iranian Bahá'ís get their act together; He invited Bahá'ís to participate with other Bahá'ís in the strengthening of a community.

What struck Dr Arbab in Colombia, he wrote, was not the material poverty he saw, but the wealth of talent that went uncultivated. A community's most important resources are its people.

Community Involvement

The key to successful community development is making community members a part of the process. A developer should always keep in mind that every member of the community has something to offer. In development, as in education, the goal is not to create something from nothing but to build on potential that already exists. Or, as Bahá'u'lláh explained, to reveal concealed treasures: 'The Great Being saith: Regard man as a mine rich in gems of inestimable value. Education can, alone, cause it to reveal its treasures, and enable mankind to benefit therefrom.'[4]

This is easier said than done. Whoever we are, wherever we're from, it's easy to associate the way we're used to doing things with the way things should be done. When developers go to new places, they don't just bring new technologies, they also unconsciously bring all of their own biases and prejudices.

According to *The Wall Street Journal*, this is why the International Monetary Fund had such a hard time dealing with the Asian economic collapse of the late 1990s.

Again and again, as Asia tumbled into crisis, the Fund sounded its approval of what turned into a spiral of competitive devaluations. These have by now left many Koreans unable to afford fuel even for heat and Indonesians strapped for food. The IMF has offered no precise plan for re-establishing a dependable system of money among these hard-hit economies.[5]

The problem? 'The tradition of muted voices in cloistered offices is inappropriate to the global information economy where the market needs all the information it can get. Recently the IMF produced an internal memo criticizing its own performance in Indonesia, where a $43 billion package has so far failed to stop the economic havoc.'[6]

Over the next two years Asian publications were even more scathing. 'The existence of the IMF and the World Bank is valid', read an editorial in Malaysia's *New Straits Times*. '. . . But what is disputed, even resented, is the way that both the IMF and the World Bank allow themselves to be ruled by American bourgeois thought . . .'[7]

As a result of its failures in Asia, the IMF came to agree with some of its critics. On 1 June 2000 the IMF's new managing director, Horst Kohler, said that the agency would stop 'lecturing or imposing' conditions on the countries it lent to: 'One of the lessons of the Asian crisis is that we should listen better to the people.'[8]

Using Local Ideas

Community development projects are more effective when we help people to figure things out for themselves rather than impose our own ideas on them.

In 1863 the US government decided that the Navajos were in the American settlers' way and forcibly relocated the tribe to the Bosque Redondo reservation on the banks of the Pecos River. Nine thousand Navajos struggled to farm and tend sheep beneath the shadow of the newly constructed Fort Sumner; 2000 died of pneumonia and dysentery. By 1868 the United States realized the project was a failure and sent General William Sherman at the head of a Peace Commission to figure out what was wrong and to develop a plan with the Native Americans to resolve it. As far as the United States officials were concerned, they had done everything right. They had given the Navajos land and protection. What was the problem? As General Sherman said to the Navajos' representative, Chief Barboncito:

> We have read in our books and learned from our officers that for many years, whether right or wrong, the Navajos have been at war with us and that General Carleton had removed you for the purpose of making you agriculturists – with that view the Government of the United States gave you money and built this fort to protect you until you were able to protect yourselves. We find you have done a good deal of work here in making acequias, but we find you have no farms, no herds and are now as poor as you were four years ago when the Government brought you here. Thus before we discuss what we are to do with you, we want to know what you have done in the past and what you think about your reservation here.[9]

The Navajos didn't think much of it, unfortunately. Chief Barboncito pointed out that many of his companions, once well-off, were now destitute. He himself was forced to obtain food from the US military commissary. The alkaline soil was poor for crops and the Comanches kept raiding Navajo sheep. Mexicans kept Navajos as slaves. The people were crowded together and thus less industrious.

General Sherman suggested that the Navajos move to the Indian Territory south of Kansas.

No, Barboncito insisted, what the Navajos really needed was their own land back. 'When the Navajos were first created four mountains and four rivers were pointed out to us, inside of which we should live, that was to be our country and was given to us by the first woman of the Navajo tribe. It was told to us by our forefathers, that we were never to move east of the Rio Grande or west of the San Juan rivers and I think that our coming here has been the cause of so much death among us and our animals.'[10]

The Navajos knew what it was going to take to satisfy them, and once the United States government started listening to them, it knew too. On 25 July 1868, the US Senate ratified a treaty with the tribe that returned them to their ancestral lands.[11]

Consultation

Every community has ideas and resources that can be utilized for its own development efforts. What's the best way to figure out what they are? A variation of the same type of method Sherman and Barboncito used: consultation.

The point of true consultation is to find the truth. It requires participants who are animated by love, who turn to God for inspiration and who all share the goal of finding the truth. Each participant should honestly and openly share his or her true concerns without becoming emotionally attached to the comments that are expressed. People are free to challenge and change the ideas without worrying about who presented them in the first place, even questioning ideas they themselves presented. The clash of opinions doesn't require a clash between people because they all share the same goal: to find the best solution as a group.

> He who expresses an opinion should not voice it as correct and right but set it forth as a contribution to the consensus of opinion, for the light of reality becomes apparent when two opinions coincide. A spark is produced when flint and steel come together. Man should weigh his opinions with the utmost serenity, calmness and composure. Before expressing his own views he should carefully consider the views already advanced by others. If he finds that a previously expressed opinion is more true and worthy, he should accept it immediately and not wilfully hold to an opinion of his own. By this excellent method he endeavours to arrive at unity and truth. Opposition and division are deplorable. It is better then to have the opinion of a wise, sagacious man; otherwise, contra-

diction and altercation, in which varied and divergent views are presented, will make it necessary for a judicial body to render decision upon the question. Even a majority opinion or consensus may be incorrect. A thousand people may hold to one view and be mistaken, whereas one sagacious person may be right. Therefore, true consultation is spiritual conference in the attitude and atmosphere of love. Members must love each other in the spirit of fellowship in order that good results may be forthcoming. Love and fellowship are the foundation.[12]

So they (members) must confer and consult in such a way that neither disagreement nor abhorrence may occur. When meeting for consultation, each must use perfect liberty in stating his views and unveiling the proof of his demonstration. If another contradicts him, he must not become excited because if there be no investigation or verification of questions and matters, the agreeable view will not be discovered neither understood. The brilliant light which comes from the collision of thoughts is the 'lightener' of facts.[13]

Consultation means coming forward to speak the truth no matter how unpopular it is or how many people or organizations have a different view. It also means being ready to adapt our views to new information when it comes to light and accepting the right of communities and elected institutions to chart their own courses regardless of whether or not they share our opinions.

The Bahá'í Administrative Order uses consultation to glean ideas from individual community members and channel them to people who can use them. Let's consider a hypothetical case, not necessarily because it's likely that a single idea will follow this precise series of events, but to illustrate the way that the Administrative Order is sustained by consultation at the grassroots.

Every month each local Bahá'í community comes together for the 19 Day Feast. The Feast is an opportunity for people to worship and socialize together and it's also a place where they consult on the affairs of the community. A 13 year old girl and a 75 year old man can both share their thoughts on the same pressing community issue. Because of the difference of their perspectives, it's quite possible that the idea generated by their dialogue will evolve into something with a wider applicability than either one of them might have come up with on their own.

Every year, when delegates are elected to go to the National Convention and vote for the National Spiritual Assembly, they're not just there for the election. They're also there to consult on the needs of their communities. So at the convention there's a possibility that the idea that was developed at the Feast will be presented and shared among the members of several cities and towns.

At the National Convention, there is 'a full, frank and unhampered consultation between the national Assembly and the assembled delegates.'[14] And every five years, when the members of the National Spiritual Assemblies gather to elect the Universal House of Justice, they consult on the state of their countries and it is possible, if statistically unlikely, that the idea that was born at Feast can now reach a global audience and inform the thoughts of people from every continent.

One of the benefits of consultation is that, by adding more information and new perspectives, it helps people find solutions to problems they might not have discovered on their own.

James Surowiecki writes a business column for *The New Yorker*. In the course of his work he discovered something very interesting: groups of people make better decisions than individuals do. Not just groups of exceptionally smart or well-educated people but groups of people of varying abilities make consistently better decisions than trained and experienced experts.

Surowiecki's book *The Wisdom of Crowds* is filled with examples. When 800 butchers, farmers, clerks and other passers-by at the 1906 West of England Fat Stock and Poultry Exhibition guessed what the weight of a particular ox would be after it had been slaughtered and dressed, the group's average guess was 1,197 pounds. The actual weight was 1,198 pounds. When the space shuttle *Challenger* exploded in 1986, the only company associated with the shuttle whose stock showed a significant decrease by the end of the day – over ten per cent – was Morton Thiokol. It was not revealed until six months later that a problem with Thiokol's O-ring seals on the booster rockets had led to the disaster and even Thiokol's executives seemed not to have anticipated this conclusion, since they hadn't tried to dump their stock. The group of investors somehow seemed to have known through its collective perceptions what no individual knew on his or her own.

However, Surowiecki's book also has a lot of examples of groups of people doing stupid things. He lists three factors that contribute to a 'smart' crowd. First, there has to be a diversity of opinion. Second, people's decisions have to be independent, which means that they're not just relying on the opinions of the people around them. And third, there has to be aggregation: some means by which everyone's private judgements can be brought together into a collective decision.[15]

In other words, groups of people can be better than individuals at solving certain types of problems but only when they interact in ways that both capitalize on and harmonize their individual strengths. Consultation fosters conditions which allow groups to work at their best.

In addition to helping the participants find truth and come to conclusions, consultation has other important roles. It creates in people the sense that they can influence their futures and don't have to wait for an outside source to provide them with direction. It inspires them with the recognition that they have ideas worth listening to. This empowerment can have consequences far beyond the specific issue being considered by the consultation itself.[16]

'Development is concerned with capacity-building at all levels of society,' says Matt Weinberg, former director of the Institute for Studies in Global Prosperity, a research agency of the Bahá'í International Community. 'A meaningful process of capacity-building manifests itself when individuals and communities begin to directly trace out their own path of development. In this regard, consultation serves as an essential tool for understanding issues, developing solutions and assessing constructive avenues of action. For Bahá'ís, consultation is the ideal mechanism of participatory learning; it is the expression of a community's true voice – the voice of equity and justice – and, thus, is a cornerstone of social well-being.'[17]

In the mid-1990s, with Afghanistan ravaged by 18 years of a war that showed no signs of slowing, the United Nations Centre for Human Settlements (UNCHS) started a development project in the city of Mazar-i-Sharif. The city had not been physically attacked but owing to the war inflation was skyrocketing, the infrastructure was overloaded and social services were virtually non-existent. Representatives of the UNCHS met with the city's men to figure out how the community could be improved but they didn't seem to be making any progress. Then they asked to speak with the women. The men told them that the women were too busy with their domestic chores to participate and, anyway, there was nothing they could say that the men hadn't already shared.

After this had been going on for weeks, Samantha Reynolds, a worker with UNHCS, again hinted that she would like to speak to women. This time, the mullah she was talking to responded by setting up a meeting.

When the women arrived, 'There were complaints and accusations. Why had the UN not consulted with them before? Why did the people in white cars [from the UN] only ever talk to men? Why was the world not helping Afghanistan? Why did the UN peace mission not talk to women? Why was there no clinic in their area? No school, no books, no salaries for teachers?'

Reynolds and other members of the UNCHS began consulting with the women about what could be done to solve the city's humanitarian crisis, which was the result of a lack of civic structure. These consultations led to the establishment of community forums. Partly businesses which contributed most of their income to community funds and partly opportunities for all the members of a community to get together every three weeks to set and work towards common goals, they were remarkably successful.

'In time, there was enough to pay for key services such as a clinic, dispensary, literacy course, library and kindergartens,' Reynolds wrote.

Extra rooms in the house were used to run educational and vocational training courses. The women ran the Forum themselves through a management committee. They established systems of administration and management, both financial and logistical, strengthening their capacity to take on wider responsibilities related to public infrastructure, such as water supplies, solid waste collection and maintenance of drains.[18]

Local Responsibility

Lasting community change takes place on the community level. It can't be imposed from above. The community members who will be affected by a plan should be involved in its implementation and kept informed of its progress.

'My experience has been that if there is not 100 per cent buy-in from the community that will be receiving the grant, you will have long-term difficulties,' says Sabine Schuller, Program Coordinator at the Rotary Foundation in Evanston, Illinois. 'For example, if there is a proposed water project in Haiti and the Haitians believe that education is a higher priority than water, you will not have a completely successful water project because not everyone's priorities are in agreement.'[19]

The government of India sets up booths in rural areas to give villagers free vaccinations. It sounds like a great idea but many villagers stay away because the idea of getting injected with a disease doesn't appeal to them. So staff from the Rabbani Bahá'í School go to villages and share information about health and hygiene along with vaccinations.

Health workers should explain the vaccination process to the people they're serving, says Dr Nicole Mohajer, head of the school's health and community outreach programmes. 'It can seem very strange or frightening because people come in and give them shots which make them feel sick or sore – it's a strange concept that you need to be injected with a disease so that you don't get it later. But it's very important to get vaccinated for a disease for which there is no medicine.'[20]

All of the school's outreach programmes, in fact, are based on the desires of the community members who will be targeted by them. Teachers at Rabbani schedule morals classes for children with residents of each surrounding community. Community members decide which classes they want and when they want them. If they don't want classes, none are set up. The focus is on the organic growth of the community and helping it to take responsibility for its own needs.

India's Mahila Samakhya programme took three years to spread from three initial states to 100,000 women in 7,335 villages in eight states. Mahila Samakhya, started with Dutch support and a variety of funding sources, encourages women to start their own *sanghas* ('groups') to educate themselves and figure out how to develop themselves and their communities. No ideas are imposed from outside; the female participants use their own insights to tackle pressing issues. 'Its non-negotiable principles include the following: respect for women's existing knowledge, experience and skills; groups at the village level set the pace, priorities, form and content of all project activities; all planning, decision-making and evaluation processes are accountable to the collective at the village level; all project structures and personnel play facilitative and supportive, rather than directive, roles.'[21] Women in the groups have learned to read and write and have familiarized themselves with their legal rights.

In one community the government's local rural development unit had been selling the kerosene entitlements for untouchable women to more prosperous buyers. But after the women organized themselves into a *sangha*, all the theft ended.

Local Spiritual Assemblies

Ideally, power shouldn't be in the hands of ambitious individuals but in elected bodies established through a voting system which minimizes as much as possible the influence of vested interests. Decisions should be made at the grassroots level, as close as possible to the people whose lives the decisions actually affect. In the

Bahá'í Faith, this ideal is found in local spiritual assemblies, which are elected annually in about 12,000 communities throughout the world.

In the Kitáb-i-Aqdas, Bahá'u'lláh gives a description of the Houses of Justice into which local spiritual assemblies are intended to evolve:

> They should consider themselves as entering the Court of the presence of God, the Exalted, the Most High, and as beholding Him Who is the Unseen. It behoveth them to be the trusted ones of the Merciful among men and to regard themselves as the guardians appointed of God for all that dwell on earth. It is incumbent upon them to take counsel together and to have regard for the interests of the servants of God, for His sake, even as they regard their own interests, and to choose that which is meet and seemly.[22]

Spiritual assemblies are the institutions which give concrete expression to the empowering principles in Bahá'u'lláh's writings.

In 1986 thousands of Khmer and Vietnamese Bahá'í refugees were being held with tens of thousands of their countrymen in border camps in Thailand. They had been displaced by regional conflicts, their safety was in jeopardy and their resources were extremely limited. Despite these difficulties, with the assistance of representatives from the Spiritual Assembly of the Bahá'ís of Thailand, the Bahá'ís in the border camps were able to elect their own local spiritual assemblies. These assemblies established schools to teach literacy and foreign language classes which were attended by refugees of all faiths. The assemblies received permission from camp authorities to build community centres and determined ways to better organize their communities and ask for support for the process of refugee resettlement.

5

Initiating Projects

Organizational Essentials

The Badí' Foundation is a non-profit organization based in Macau with three projects: the School of the Nations; a centre for curriculum development which helps develop curriculum and train teachers for the School of Nations, among other activities; and the Social Enterprise Program which helps initiate social service projects and includes programmes on environmental action and enhancing learning environments. The Badí' Foundation also has a consultancy programme which provides expertise to agencies such as UNDP and UNICEF and also helps non-governmental organizations and international agencies run its programmes themselves in their own countries.

Dr Noguchi, Badí''s president, says that three actions were crucial for the foundation's growth and are essential for successful and sustainable social and economic development organizations in general:

1) Focus

It is extremely important to focus your resources and energies. So many worthwhile projects and possible lines of action arise that it is very easy for energies to be diffused. Having a clear mission statement and vision of how your organization will contribute is very important because it helps you make decisions about what you won't do, and that is often just as important as the decisions about what you will do.

2) Find the right people

Also, it is very important to be clear about what the needs are for a specific position, so that you do not employ people who are great people but who don't have the skills you need.

3) Refine your vision

Likewise, it is important that you are constantly building and refining your vision as an organization and that you choose people who want to work within the framework and vision that the organization has chosen. There are many different approaches that Bahá'í-inspired organizations can take to learning to apply the teachings to social and economic development, and groups that work together need to have a compatible approach.[1]

Health for Humanity, an Illinois-based organization, works to eradicate river blindness in Cameroon, helps to make modern cataract surgery available in Albania, is developing a plan to combat preventable blindness in Mongolia, provides health education in China, helps Núr University to strengthen its public health programme in Bolivia, is raising awareness of HIV/AIDS prevention with the Varqa Foundation in Guyana, helps teach conflict resolution to California schoolchildren, and is running a smoking prevention campaign in Ohio. How does it get so much done? By using an eight-step process:

1) Information-gathering with local and national communities to learn about their needs and problems.

2) Facilitating problem-solving by using collective decision-making to reach a unified plan that is culturally appropriate and addresses local needs.

3) Encouraging people at the grassroots level to commit to the project and take a proactive role in problem-solving.

4) Helping to organize necessary resources and expertise by nurturing and relying upon the desire to be of service that motivates so many people.

5) Aiding networking to marshal resources.

6) Providing educational materials, equipment, training and supplies as needed.

7) Establishing collaborative and respectful relationships with individuals and institutions to reach established goals.

8) Promoting the recognition that social and economic development must rest on universal ethical principles such as the equality of women and men, trustworthiness and unity.[2]

Vision

Every project and organization needs a vision. As a letter written on behalf of Shoghi Effendi explains, 'we as Bahá'ís must first clearly define the issue involved, set our goal before us, and work wisely, persistently and patiently towards its accomplishment'.[3]

The vision should be clearly spelled out in an organization's vision statement. This statement will make sure that everyone is working in unity towards the same goals and it will also let people outside of the organization understand what the organization hopes to accomplish.

Health for Humanity has a 'Grant Proposal Planning Guide' that helps organizations formulate a vision by answering a series of questions.

First, what specific issues do we want our project to address?

Second, what are the project's specific goals and objectives? In other words, what do we intend it to accomplish?

'The answers to these two questions need to be written down,' says Verderoon. 'Everyone needs to be on the same page, literally.'

Third, we should describe the population that we hope to benefit from the project. What are their ages, their locations, the number of people we intend to reach?

Fourth, what are the specific activities and events that will take place through our proposed project? We should thoroughly explain exactly what we're going to do.

Fifth, in what specific ways do these activities and events address the issues identified in the first question? 'You should be able to acknowledge what hasn't worked or build on something that has,' Verderoon says.

Sixth, we should define the time period over which these activities will take place.[4]

These ideas can provide a starting point for the development of our vision statements. Mission statements can be simple, like this one from the Mona Foundation:

> Mona Foundation is a non-profit charitable organization dedicated to supporting grassroots educational initiatives, and raising the status of women and girls in the United States and abroad.[5]

Or more in-depth, such as Health for Humanity's statement:

> Health for Humanity, a volunteer-based organization, strengthens capacities for health development by applying universal moral principles and scientific strategies. HH is a health development organization established in 1992. HH endeavours to encourage harmony and cooperation, incorporating into all projects a belief that the human race is one family that is inherently noble, and that people everywhere have the capacity to direct their own progress. HH facilitates grassroots health development through partnership with local institutions focused on training and building capacity. The human and financial resources of HH come from Members, Supporters and Partners throughout the world . . .[6]

Commitment

Sustainability requires a long-term commitment. As Health for Humanity explains:

> Health for Humanity has learned, in more than a decade of experience, that health development requires long-term commitment and patience. The kind of fundamental change and development of capacity that HH seeks to establish cannot occur quickly. Short-term projects, while beneficial to the few individuals they may impact, rarely yield long-term results. Therefore, HH projects aimed at health development require a minimum of three to five years of commitment, preferably longer. Furthermore, projects that focus on service delivery, while valuable, especially in times of disaster, do not develop local capacity or enduring change. HH's focus is on the development of capacity and sustainability. The best approach for any particular area tends to evolve through mutual, respectful partnerships, with local partners providing the leadership as well as the intended outcomes of development. Therefore institutional partnerships that HH develops tend to be long-lasting, reciprocal, and based on mutual respect.[7]

Structure

The Baháʼí Office of Social and Economic Development has determined that a clearly-defined governance structure is conducive to efficient decision-making and action in a community development organization. In Health for Humanity, for example, general policy is decided by a board of directors, while the policy's implementation is guided by an executive director and day-to-day affairs are conducted by paid and volunteer staff. The board solicits input from every level of the organization but also lets the staff spend most of its time in direct service, not administration. Health for Humanity strives to have a simple and efficient organization, with most of the paid jobs focusing on project support, volunteer placement and financial growth.

In the vision section above, we started asking questions about our project's focus and goals. Now it's time to consider the people who will be responsible for making sure these goals get carried out. Who will plan, organize and implement the organization's activities and what will their roles and responsibilities be? What qualifications do these individuals possess?

These questions will become particularly important if we intend to seek grants. 'Even if you've got the greatest idea in the world,' Verderoon says, 'grant funders want a sure thing and they try to guarantee that by getting people who are qualified . . . If you have an education programme and you're not an education professional, you'd better get one.' When it comes time to list team members' qualifications in a grant proposal, 'throw all modesty aside'.[8]

It's important to be aware that as non-profit organizations become bigger and seek larger grants, funding organizations will take a greater interest in the composition of their boards of directors. One particular area they will concern themselves with is what percentage of the funds raised by the organization come through the board itself, by members who raise funds on their own or make their own contributions. Most foundations consider strong board support to be crucial to fundraising and if they don't see it, they will sometimes ask that changes be made to the board. Foundations understand the need for community governance but traditional foundations also say, overtly or implicitly, 'If your board's not supporting you financially, why should we?' It's not uncommon for large organizations to have boards of directors with 50 members, all looking for resources in different places.

A new non-profit organization with a local focus will generally look for board members in two places. First, it will seek out community stakeholders, people who care about their communities, are actively engaged in community issues and are respected locally. These individuals are usually easy to find. Second, its founders will ask the straightforward question, 'Who do we know who has access to resources?' Where do you bank? Who is your doctor? Who represents you legally? Who does your audits? (Non-profit organizations in the United States, as in many countries, are required to have audits.) Who are the local business leaders? If there are no big businesses around, who owns the local restaurant franchise? Even in poor communities someone owns the buildings and there might be well-off individuals who grew up in the area and now live elsewhere.

Non-profit organizers don't normally invite people onto the board at the first meeting. They sit down and get to know them. They explain that they're part of a community group that's looking for ideas on how to improve the area. They ask them why they have put their businesses where they have. Verderoon makes it clear that during these initial meetings he's not going to accept their money even if it's offered; he's meeting them for their advice and counsel about community issues.[9]

In general terms, everyone on the board of directors should be deeply committed to the issues facing the organization. Some of them will be experts in the field and some of them will be adept at finding resources and developing organizations.

Another important consideration for social and economic development projects is volunteers, which many projects rely upon. Volunteers should be given clear descriptions of their duties, receive orientation and training, and be regularly checked up on to make sure that they're being provided with adequate support.

Accountability

Everyone in an organization should have standards that they understand and for which they are held accountable.

'In a non-profit organization there have to be mechanisms for accountability for volunteers,' says Layli Miller-Muro, founder and Executive Director of the Tahirih Justice Center. 'For example, the board of directors has to be made responsible. If you're on a board of directors of a place where people's lives are at stake, if you promise to look into legal liability insurance and you don't,[10] there are real consequences. There needs to be a culture of accountability.'[11] Accountability is not by any means limited to individuals.

To be effective and make sure that they are fulfilling their goals, organizations have to hold themselves accountable to the people they serve and who are impacted by their actions.

This is true even for organizations that don't define themselves primarily as altruistic. The Ford website states,

> Our stakeholders – those who affect Ford or are affected by us – are numerous. A closer look, however, shows that we have sustained, interdependent relationships with several distinct categories of stakeholders: our employees, customers, dealers, suppliers, investors and communities. Also important is our relationship to 'society', including government, nongovernmental organizations (NGOs) and academia.[12]

Because some of Ford's actions affected things they cared about, these stakeholders weren't always content to be mere observers. According to Ford's website:

> Some shareholders have submitted concerns directly to the Company. In 2003, shareholders contacted us regarding the reduction of greenhouse gas emissions, HIV/AIDS and several governance issues . . . St Joseph Health System and other shareholder proponents submitted a shareholder proposal requesting a reporting of our policies and actions to address the global HIV/AIDS pandemic.[13]

After this, Ford became more proactive in seeking that stakeholder's advice: 'In addition, we have solicited the involvement of St Joseph Health System in the process of developing and implementing our approach to HIV/AIDS.'[14]

The One World Trust, an organization that promotes education and research into the changes within global organizations that would lead to the eradication of poverty, injustice and war, explains in a discussion of its framework for facilitating organizational accountability that

. . . accountability is defined not only as a means through which individuals and organizations are held responsible for their decisions and actions, but also as a means by which they take internal responsibility for shaping their organizational mission and values, for opening themselves to external scrutiny and for assessing performance in relation to goals.[15]

What are some of the ways to make organizations more accountable? First of all, they have to be 'transparent'. People, particularly stakeholders, need to be able to see how they work and what they're doing. Such organizations continually measure, report on and improve their performance in all areas. (Some keys to effective measurement are explored below, in the sections on 'Evaluation' and 'Benchmarks of Progress'.) Accountable organizations also engage their stakeholders in assessing, reporting on and helping to implement their activities.[16] (The importance of grassroots and stakeholder involvement is considered in much of this chapter, beginning with the section 'True Development'.)

A Holistic Approach

In 1905 Albert Einstein proposed the special theory of relativity, which includes the famous formula $E=mc^2$. Ten years later, in 1915, he put forward a general theory of relativity, which presented a new, non-Newtonian explanation of gravity based on the curvature of space–time. Many physicists have speculated that if Einstein had known more about geometry, specifically Bernhard Riemann's work on spherical geometry in the 1850s and William Clifford's ideas about space curvature in the 1870s, 'he could very well have come up with the general theory soon after he developed the special theory,' according to science writer John Gribbin.[17]

Interdisciplinary approaches can help people solve social problems more efficiently, too, and the Bahá'í International Community has stressed that interdisciplinary action is necessary for significant progress. While isolated projects 'can yield tangible results, experience worldwide amply demonstrates that fragmented activities in health, education, agriculture, and so on will not lead to sustainable development'.

> No one discipline can offer solutions to all the problems besetting humanity. Effective development unequivocally calls for coordinated interdisciplinary and multisectoral action. Organizational structures capable of dealing with increasing degrees of theoretical and administrative complexity are needed to integrate efforts across various fields and to provide the coherence required for consistent advance.[18]

The Women's Legal Rights Initiative is a project in India that draws from a variety of disciplines to advance the status of women. 'There are a lot of economic empowerment linkages,' says Vasu Mohan of the initiative. 'A link between economic empowerment and legal rights, a link between economic empowerment and literacy.'[19]

The Women's Legal Rights Initiative is representative of many community development projects in that it contains a few cross-disciplinary collaborations rather than a completely holistic approach. 'There are lots of examples [of] linkages that are more project to project and organization to organization [than a consideration of] what are the roots of this problem and how can they be approached,' Mohan says.[20]

Building Capacity

The document 'Bahá'í Social and Economic Development' recommends that projects start with 'a relatively simple set of actions' that can be sustained and from which the community can learn. As the people involved in the project gain capacity and learn from their activities, 'complexity will arise naturally in an organic way'.[21]

The Bahá'í International Community, in '. . . *for the betterment of the world*', outlines a strategy for a development project's growth.

1) A community perceives a need and has the desire to address it.

2) A simple set of actions is developed that can be managed by the community itself.

3) '. . . participants achieve success, gain experience, and increase their capacity to make decisions about their spiritual and material progress and implement them.'

4) 'Local action gives rise to projects of a more sustained nature with more ambitious goals. Invariably, organizational structures are created to support such projects, and some of these nascent agencies possess the potential to evolve into fully fledged development organizations with the ability to undertake programmes in a wide field of action.'[22]

Levels of Complexity

The Office of Social and Economic Development at the Bahá'í World Centre currently distinguishes among development projects according to three levels of complexity:[23]

- Activities of fixed duration, from health camps to tree-planting, are relatively simple efforts to apply spiritual principles to the problems that Bahá'ís face in their communities.
- Sustained projects are usually 'administered by nascent development organizations which have the potential to grow in complexity' and influence.
- Advanced projects have the capacity to undertake complex action. They 'systematically train human resources' and normally manage multiple 'lines of action' to address community needs in a coordinated, multi-disciplinary manner.

Evaluation

The Bahá'í International Community lists six steps in what it calls 'a distinctly Bahá'í approach' to social and economic development:[24]

1) fostering and supporting action

2) reflection on action

3) study

4) consultation

5) the systematization of experience

6) training

The project requires action, the actions are evaluated and in a consultative process those actions are refined and systematized. People are trained to carry the actions forward. The evaluation, or 'reflection on action', is an activity applying Bahá'u'lláh's injunction to 'Bring thyself to account each day'[25] to the project itself.

In order for this process to work, an organization needs to have goals, which are encapsulated in its vision statement. It will also need to have benchmarks or indicators to let it know whether its goals are being met.

If our goal is to achieve literacy within a specified population, for example, an indicator might be when a certain percentage of the population is able to read at a particular level. Goals should be realistic and based on a study of the situation and consultation with the community; in this example, for instance, we would need to know the population's reading levels before beginning the project.

'Learning in this sense is not limited to study and evaluation,' the 'Bahá'í Social and Economic Development' document states. 'It comes about in combination with action. The believers must regularly engage in consultation, action, reflection – all in the light of the guidance inherent in the Teachings of the Faith.'[26]

The Tahirih Justice Center engages in a process of continual reflection and refinement. First, it conducts an annual strategic planning process that relies on consultation-based decision-making. The Center's overall plan is then given to its staff members, who make their own long-term goals based on the Center's broader agenda.

The Center's planning process is informed by constant feedback. The staff is reviewed every three months; staff members review their peers, their supervisors and the people they are supervising.

Vasu Mohan uses outside evaluators for his projects. 'We also often form an advisory group, a partnership of NGOs, that we constantly go back to, to make sure everything is on track,' he explains.[27]

Jeffrey Hollender is the President and CEO of Seventh Generation, the United States's leading brand of natural household products and a company that takes pride in its commitment to social responsibility. At a talk at Northwestern University in March 2004, Mr Hollender explained that Seventh Generation considers outside evaluation to be critical to its product and organizational improvement. 'If you don't subject yourself to outside evaluation, it's almost impossible to know where your biggest adverse impacts and opportunities are,' he said.[28]

As an example, Hollender told the audience of a time when Seventh Generation had brought in an outside consultant to determine where the company was causing the most harm. After the consultant looked at every aspect of the business, he determined that the company's biggest adverse impact was the energy used and the CO_2 released when customers heated their cleaning products.

This came as a complete surprise. 'It wasn't even on our list of problems,' Hollender said. Based on the new information, Seventh Generation reformulated its cleaning products to work as well in cold water as in hot.[29]

Benchmarks of Progress

Outcomes

Organizations need benchmarks, or standards, by which they can judge their progress. The ability to track progress against benchmarks is crucial to receiving continued funding from donor agencies, to creating a sustainable programme and to simply making sure that the organization is doing what it is meant to do.

In order to create useful benchmarks, we need to address at least three questions:

1) Whom are we going to serve?

2) What are the needs of this target group and which needs will we address?

3) How will the programme address these needs? In other words, what services will we offer?

An organization can't be all things to all people. It will have to focus. In its literature and outreach it should also avoid creating unrealistic expectations. The goal for a new organization should be to provide quality services in one particular area.

Once the initial three questions have been answered, it's time for a fourth:

4) What will clients gain at the end of the programme and what will a 'successful' client look like?

The benefits provided by a programme can range from those that are concrete and easy to measure, such as a health checkup for each person, to those which are more abstract and complex, such as an improved understanding by clients of the relationship between health and lifestyle.[30]

These goals or benchmarks are often called targets and the data that are used to evaluate progress against the targets are called indicators. The former, quantitative goals can be referred to as outputs, while the latter, qualitative goals are sometimes known as outcomes. Outputs tell us how much of something we have done and how often, while outcomes refer to how people have developed as a result of our efforts and what they go on to do afterwards.

United Way of America, an organization dedicated to improving people's lives by mobilizing the caring power of communities, encourages health and human services organizations to measure outcomes along with outputs, so that they can determine how much of an impact their programmes are actually making in people's lives.[31]

'Rarely can an indicator stand alone as a meaningful source of information,' the Bahá'í International Community states in the document *Valuing Spirituality in Development*. 'Progress is not an event or a statistic, but a process – a trend made up of numerous factors. It cannot be expressed by one measure or by reference to a single point in time. Indicators must, therefore, be placed in a specific temporal context and correlated with measures of other related factors.'[32]

Project management should include both monitoring and evaluation, which are two distinct activities. Monitoring is a constant process of observation to make sure that the project is heading in the right direction. Evaluations are assessments of how closely the projects are meeting their stated objectives. Before we can begin an evaluation, we'll need to make sure that our goals are clearly stated. These goals should be linked to relevant, measurable indicators, in the form of outputs and outcomes we intend to reach by certain times, to allow us to determine whether or not our goals are being achieved.

Different organizations use different models to map the relationships between their indicators. What all the models should have in common is the ability to express what people expect to put into a project and what they expect to get out.

Let's use one popular planning and evaluation tool, the 'logic model', as an example. The logic model below was adapted by

R. Weslie Ellison, a research consultant, from a matrix used by the World Bank Institute Evaluation Group. This model has five components: the input, or the resources that go into the project; the activities, which are what the project does; anticipated outputs; anticipated outcomes; and anticipated impacts, which are long-term, system-wide changes on a community level.[33]

Models are useful because they explicitly state the organizers' assumptions about what the project participants hope to achieve and provide a basis for evaluating whether they're meeting these goals or not. They can be important tools in the development, management and evaluation of projects.

How do we decide what outputs and outcomes to use as indicators? Development practitioners often use the 'CREAM' rule to identify indicators which will be useful and practical to measure. According to this rule, indicators should be:

- clear (precise and unambiguous)
- relevant (clearly related to the stated goal)
- economic (able to be measured at a reasonable cost)
- adequate (capable of providing a sufficient basis to assess performance)
- monitorable (amenable to independent validation)[34]

But there's something else we should be looking at as well, and that's how closely the indicators are connected to our project's ultimate mission. In *Valuing Spirituality in Development*, the Bahá'í International Community articulates a strategy for formulating indicators based on spiritual principles: 'The components of a spiritually based indicator include a vision of a peaceful and united future; the selected principle(s) crucial to the realization of that future; the policy area addressed by the principle(s); and the goal toward which the measure assesses progress. The indicator is quantitatively or qualitatively measurable and verifiable, and it is adaptable within a wide diversity of contexts without violating the integrity of the principle(s) involved.'[35]

Logic Model Matrix

Input	Activities	Outputs	Outcomes	Impact
Resources: people, money, books, facilities, etc.	**What the programme does:** trains people, provides services	**Products and services:** a calculation of effort and activity	**Benefits to participants:** short-term results	**Long-term effects:** achievement of long-term goals
Examples: The people and institutions that support the programme's activities Where the programme is held The amount of money that is spent on the project Material resources, such as information technology systems, literature and educational aids The key professional and vocational skills, spiritual qualities and other attributes which volunteers and staff will need to perform their duties	Types of services • literacy training • moral development • health services Training of human resources	Number of people served Number of volunteers trained to perform functions of the project Number of new programmes Results of efforts that are performed • participatory learning • grassroots action • organic growth • consultation skills	Fostering moral and material advancement Presence of community voice Increased empowerment and capacity Creation of atmosphere of: • dignity • optimism • commitment • awareness and understanding Creation of new patterns of social interaction Increased number of trained volunteers Achieving measurable and quantifiable outcomes • youth who have successfully completed a training programme • success in building a coalition of agencies	Fostering social transformation • unity in diversity • equity and justice • equality of the sexes • trustworthiness and moral leadership • independent investigation of truth

This means that those of us who wish to draw on the benefits of spiritually based indicators have a lot to consider: a positive vision of the future, a recognition of the spiritual principles consummated in that vision and an understanding of how those principles might be applied in practical ways to the world we live in.

True Development

The goal of development is to help people learn how to improve some aspect of their lives. Unfortunately, development projects face the risk of being misled by conventional terminology before they've even had the chance to get started. We call some countries 'developed' and others 'developing', which implies that the goal of development is to make certain countries look more like certain other countries. Usually, since the most obvious difference between developed and developing countries seems to be wealth, the result is to measure progress solely in economic terms. However, social relationships can also be important indicators of a community's health. Holly Hanson, a professor of History and African and African-American Studies at Mt Holyoke College, made this point clear in a talk at the 2000 Bahá'í Social and Economic Development Conference in Florida:

> In order to think about economics clearly, it is useful to keep in mind that production always has social as well as material dimensions. All economic activity creates social relationships. Every time a person makes something, or adds value to something, or buys or sells something, that action has material and social consequences . . . Every economic activity we engage in, when we are producing things, adding value to things or exchanging things, creates opportunities to express love, concern and respect for other people. The more this happens, the more vital the connections will be, and also, the more prosperous . . . The opposite is also true. Economic activity which does not recognize the interdependence of all participants, which expresses self-interest rather than concern for others, is not only not productive, it is

utterly, essentially destructive. Over the long term, self-interested economic activity creates differences that engender hatred and social disorder.[36]

Development must be social as well as economic: it must help people learn how to build relationships that are conducive to their overall prosperity.

Dr Cornell Menking learned from experience that development projects need to focus on more than the transfer of material goods to succeed. 'In 1988 I joined the Peace Corps,' he writes. 'I frequently tell a story from those days to illustrate the problem that has driven me since it occurred in a small, West African village in Sierra Leone.

> I was working for a United Nations project as an agriculture extension agent. The first time I met my Dutch supervisor he showed me a letter he had written: a scathing report of the destructive impact the project was having on the local economy and social structure. For example, it illustrated how the outboard motors and fishing nets, provided to villagers on credit which was never actually paid back, was creating a psychology of dependency. The letter also explained how 'inappropriate technology' was undermining the local economy by unfairly subsidizing a limited number of local fishermen, as well as creating greed and animosity among them.
>
> It was a beautiful letter and I was immediately proud to work with a principled leader who had the moral courage to send this to his superiors. But he was new on the job. A few months later, after seeing first hand how the concerns he had raised were quite accurate, I asked him what happened with the letter. 'Oh, I never sent it,' was his reply. He explained that if he had sent it the entire project probably would have been shut down and everyone would be out of work.
>
> The Peace Corps Volunteers were disillusioned, to say the least. Our director was more concerned with his own well-being, unready to sacrifice his wind-surfer, beautiful home, Land Cruiser and personal servants – all of which existed in an extremely poor

village. He also found it quite easy – on paper – to show that the project was achieving results economically.

I happen to know that now, 13 years later, there is no evidence of any 'development' having taken place in that village because this entire population was displaced to Guinean refugee camps due to civil war.[37]

Development organizations should evaluate the social impact of their actions but this evaluation shouldn't be confined to them. At his talk at Northwestern University, Hollender suggested that businesses should track their progress against values-based as well as economic benchmarks – not only because it was the right thing to do but because it would ultimately make them more sustainable.[38] This helps explain why Dr Diamond found that Chevron was operating an oil field in Papua New Guinea with so much concern for the environment that animal species seemed more abundant within the field than outside of it. Dr Diamond described the reasoning in his book *Collapse*:

> Chevron and some of the other large international oil companies
> . . . realized that, by spending each year an extra few million dollars on a project, or even a few tens of millions of dollars, they
> would save money in the long run by minimizing the risk of
> losing billions of dollars in . . . an accident, or of having an entire
> project closed down and losing its whole investment.[39]

Social relationships are an indicator of community health and a culture of values can be used to gauge a business's strength.[40]

In the *Journal of Bahá'í Studies*, Anna C. Vakil draws on Bahá'u'lláh's writings to identify an even more basic component of true development: human dignity. All human beings need dignified lives, she states, and all human beings are capable of striving for them. Any new theory of development must be based on this striving because without dignity no material fix will ever be sufficient. The primary engine for achieving dignity is the human will.[41]

The awakening, inspiration and cultivation of the human will on an individual and collective level, then, can perhaps be seen as one of the best ways to effect positive change.

The Bellagio Principles for Assessment

In 1987 the World Commission on Environment and Development, also known as the Brundtland Commission, called for development practitioners to come up with new methods for measuring the progress of sustainable development initiatives. One response came in November 1996, when development practitioners and researchers from around the world met at the Rockefeller Foundation's Study and Conference Centre in Bellagio, Italy, at the invitation of the International Institute for Sustainable Development. They unanimously agreed on what have come to be called the Bellagio Principles for Assessment.

1) The assessment of progress towards sustainable development should be guided by a clear vision and well-understood goals.

2) The assessment should be holistic, reviewing the whole system and the parts that make it up, including social, ecological and economic subsystems. The assessment should consider both negative and positive consequences of human activity, on both human and ecological systems, and in both financial and non-monetary terms.

3) The assessment should consider the system's essential elements, such as equity and disparity within the current population and between the current and future generations; ecological conditions; and economic and other, non-market activities that contribute to human well-being.

4) The assessment should be of adequate scope. It should consider a time frame long enough for the evaluation of impacts on future generations as well as short-term needs and an area large enough

for the evaluation of impacts on distant people and ecosystems. It should build on historic and contemporary conditions while anticipating future conditions.

5) The assessment should have a practical focus. The vision and goals should be linked to specific indicators and the number of indicators should be limited to provide for a clear recognition of progress. Measurement should be standardized whenever possible to facilitate comparisons.

6) The assessment should be pursued in a spirit of openness. The methods and data should be accessible to everyone. Judgements, assumptions, and uncertainties in the data and interpretations of the data should be made explicit.

7) The assessment should be effectively communicated. It should be designed to address the needs of the audience. It should draw from indicators that are designed to engage and stimulate decision-makers. The results should be communicated clearly and plainly.

8) There should be broad representation in the assessment team. Key grassroots, professional, technical and social groups should be represented, including youth, women and indigenous people, to ensure the inclusion of diverse and changing values. Decision-makers should also be included to make sure that the assessment leads to action and is considered in policy-making.

9) Assessment should be ongoing. Capacity should be developed for repeated measurement to track trends. Because systems are complicated and frequently change, assessments should be able to adapt accordingly. Goals, frameworks and indicators should be adjusted as new insights are gained. Collective learning and feedback for decision-making should be promoted.

10) Finally, the continuity of assessment work should be ensured through the development of institutional capacity. Responsibilities

should be clearly assigned and ongoing support should be provided for the decision-making process. Capacity should be built for data collection, maintenance and documentation. There should also be support for local assessment capacity.[42]

Learning

The Bahá'í International Community states that 'All Bahá'í projects are directed towards the visible improvement of some aspect of life.'[43]

The programme's goals can be modest or broad but it must be capable of learning from its experience. 'Every Bahá'í development project – whatever its size or scope – serves as a centre for learning that promotes material, moral, and spiritual progress. Thus, while concerted action should lead to concrete results, success is measured more in terms of the impact of action on the capacity of individuals and their communities to address development issues at increasingly higher levels of complexity and effectiveness.'[44]

In other words, a Bahá'í community development project must have clear objectives, must adapt to the knowledge its participants acquire and must help people develop the capacity to improve their own lives and environments. It is, in a word, empowering.

Dr Javid explains that the Mona Foundation funds projects that have simple, clear-to-understand metrics, have been founded by members of the community and have community support: in other words, they're not some individual's pet project.

She explains how complexity evolved at the Ruaha Secondary School in Tanzania, one of the poorest countries on the planet:

> Ruaha started as an academic school. Then they came to understand that agriculture is an essential part of [regional] community activities. Their curriculum had to adapt to that. So they started an agriculture track. Then they realized that there was a need for moral development and added that. There were no health facilities around, so they decided they needed a nursing office on their grounds.

Later, they developed 'different ways of generating income than [had been] conceived on the first day'.[45]

Development is a process. As communities learn more, they develop their capacities, tackle larger programmes, learn from these new experiences and apply them to even greater challenges. An example of this can be seen in the evolution of the Bahá'í community itself. At a time when National Spiritual Assemblies were demonstrating new levels of confidence and achieving unprecedented successes, the Universal House of Justice called for the establishment of Regional Bahá'í Councils, which would decentralize many of the tasks of National Spiritual Assemblies. Shortly after many Bahá'ís began to develop an appreciation for the role of Regional Bahá'í Councils, the Universal House of Justice began to encourage initiatives that took place on the level of clusters of adjacent communities.

In both cases, the previous institutions weren't abandoned as communities developed; instead, they were able to focus more precisely on their primary missions. Yet every time it seemed that lessons had been learned, whenever people began to feel that they were in control of their situations, they were challenged to reach just a little bit higher. This is a culture of learning and growth – and development.

Dr Moojan Momen points out in his essay 'A Change of Culture' that when Shoghi Effendi began training Bahá'ís to implement the administrative framework envisioned and articulated by Bahá'u'lláh and 'Abdu'l-Bahá, many Bahá'ís were uncomfortable with this change to their communities. In fact, between 1916 and 1926 (Shoghi Effendi assumed the Guardianship in 1921), the US Bahá'í community declined in membership by 50 per cent (from 2,884 to 1,247 believers).[46] But by learning to form the Faith's institutions, the believers who remained were setting the stage for the community's future progress.

Whenever we experiment, it's possible that our first few attempts might not go so well. Growth, development and learning all involve risk. And risk requires courage and the ability to let go of our egos.

A Baháʾí community development project:
- is directed at the visible improvement of some aspect of life
- must be capable of learning from its experiences
- serves as a centre for learning
- promotes material, moral and spiritual progress
- measures success by the ability of individuals and their communities to address development issues at increasingly higher levels of complexity and effectiveness

Local Resources

One way to help communities achieve self-sufficiency is to help them identify indigenous or easily accessible resources.

To learn agricultural skills and work towards the goal of economic self-sufficiency, students at Rabbani School help to raise crops: the wheat that goes into their bread, for example, as well as their eggs and many vegetables, are produced on the school grounds. When the students return to their villages, they are able to immediately apply what they have learned at school to the improvement of their living circumstances.

One night, walking across the school grounds with a plate of food and a glass of water, I was struck by the realization that all the food had been grown and prepared at the school, the water had been pumped at the school well and the electricity for the lights that lit my way was being generated on site, the power from the nearby town of Gwalior having gone out earlier in the evening.

Originally, the school's soil had been too alkaline to plant crops. A native tree was planted which dropped seed pods that changed the soil composition over five years. The trees could then be cut down for firewood and the land could be farmed.

When development projects are initiated, Vasu Mohan explains, they begin with an assessment of the community's needs and resources.

More and more, we are looking at participatory processes that will affect priorities and strategies. For example, the Women's Legal Rights Initiative in India – we're bringing in NGOs that have already been engaged in this work, asking them to look at what's been done in the past, what needs to be done, what's worked, so that we cannot repeat what happened in the past but build on it. Then, we look at what kind of financial resources will be needed and external (and if it exists, internal) expertise and where will that come from.[47]

The evaluation of need comes before the allocation of resources. As Health for Humanity has noted, 'Available funding opportunities should not define project or programme priorities.'[48]

Every community, no matter how poor, has resources that can contribute to its development: its people, their knowledge and their social networks.

'Contrary to common perception, the biggest challenge of getting a social and economic development project off the ground is not related to lack of resources,' says Mojgan Sami. 'The funds are there but the processes of dissemination are complex, overly bureaucratic and usually do not reach those that are most in need of the finances.'[49] These issues have been identified by individuals, civil society, government officials and donor agencies. Although there are ongoing discussions and dialogues on 'simplifying' processes, ensuring that local communities are entrusted with development finances, cutting down on 'churning' and removing bottlenecks in financial systems, change happens slowly. Another challenge comes from the local level.

As an example, I was working on a USAID-funded project with Land 'o' Lakes International [as part of the volunteer Farmer-to-Farmer programme] in Siberia to empower a local community-based organization to obtain development funds in order to build a small business consulting centre for local producers who had just entered into a competitive 'market' system. (Having been under communism for so long, many farmers were not trained in business practices such as marketing.) On the first day of my meetings with local officials, I asked the director of the community-based organization what their goals were for the consulting centre. He replied, 'To have enough money to buy computers for our farmers.' We then entered into a discussion of why computers, who would train the farmers, were they interested, etc. The director was just concerned with how much money I could give him. I was more concerned with priority setting and enabling the director to establish a sustainable institution.

This is another challenge or myth that keeps a project from getting off the ground. Concentrating on the money keeps local officials and citizens from stocktaking, priority setting and building processes that will be sustainable and effective. It took some time for me to convince the director to call a meeting with the farmers who were part of the *rayon* (county) which would benefit from the small business consulting centre. When we were around a table together, issues of concern to the community began to arise. Issues such as improving produce, roads to the city, building a cooperative, etc. Not one of the farmers thought that having access to three computers in the business centre was a priority. This exercise allowed the director to realize that broad-based consultations, needs assessments and priority setting needed to happen on a community level before seeking development finances. This will allow local citizens to have a voice in the process of their own development. This voice empowers and energizes individuals to action and commitment to the development of the community. Without this commitment and participation, development efforts tend to fail because they are not sustainable.[50]

Conflict over Resources

Like Bahá'u'lláh, 'Abdu'l-Bahá on several occasions compared the world to a human body:

As preordained by the Fountainhead of Creation, the temple of the world hath been fashioned after the image and likeness of the human body . . . By this is meant that even as the human body in this world which is outwardly composed of different limbs and organs, is in reality a closely integrated, coherent entity, similarly the structure of the physical world is like unto a single being whose limbs and members are inseparably linked together.[51]

Professor Hanson points out that by ignoring the interconnected relationships in a community, development projects can actually cause more harm than good. "'Abdu'l-Bahá's image of the growth of social and political institutions explains why so many efforts to improve social conditions in the resource-poor parts of the world are not successful,' she stated at the 2000 Bahá'í Social and Economic Development Conference in Orlando, Florida.

The development of a human being has coherence: all the parts grow in harmony with each other . . . In contrast, schemes for social improvement that originate in one part of the world and are implemented in another part of the world lack the quality of coherence. Intended to replace or 'improve' the patterns of interaction which already exist in a community, they often ignore its power dynamics and how the project itself affects habits and structures regarding who has a voice and who does not have a voice in the region. They can serve to reinforce structures which silence some voices, or strengthen the power that some people unfairly wield over others. Because development projects almost always bring very scarce resources, they generate intense conflict over access to those resources, and those conflicts can be very damaging to the growth of patterns of broad, equitable empowerment of community members.[52]

An example of this was evident in 1999, when Shell Oil donated disused pipes in Nigeria's Delta State. The donation was an attempt to reach out to the community and improve public relations. Youth started fighting over the pipes and 60 people died. The following January a donation of $44,200 by Shell to a Delta State king was apparently misplaced (or misappropriated) by the ruler, resulting in his palace being stormed by outraged youth who beheaded him and set the palace on fire. Five people lost their lives and hundreds were seriously injured.

One of the ways to address this problem is to recognize that a community's greatest resource is the individuals who comprise it and to recognize their empowerment as the key to successful development. Bahá'u'lláh, addressing the kings of the world, stated plainly: 'Your people are your treasures.'[53]

'My understanding is that Bahá'í-sponsored SED projects are grounded in the principle that we are essentially spiritual beings,' says Dr Javid, 'and in order to develop as a species we have to work on all aspects of our education, including spiritual (this does not mean religious). One of the principles that distinguishes Bahá'í SED projects, for me, is that every person has the capacity to be the protagonist of his own development and funding agencies have to be very careful not to stifle that.'[54]

Positive Deviance

In 1990 Save the Children sent Jerry Sternin to Vietnam to start a Save the Children branch and lower malnutrition rates. Half the country's children were malnourished and he had only been given six months. He was ready to innovate.

'We call conventional wisdom about malnutrition "true but useless" or "TBU",' Sternin is quoted as saying in a *Fast Company* magazine article. 'It's all about poor sanitation, ignorance, food-distribution patterns, poverty, and a lack of access to good water. Millions of kids can't wait for those issues to be addressed. While you are there, things improve, but as soon as you leave, things revert back to the baseline.'[55]

Mr Sternin turned for a new approach to the work of Dr Marian Zeitlin. At Tufts University in the 1980s, her research had looked at the minorities, the 'deviants' who did better than their peers. Mr Sternin decided that what he needed to do in Vietnam was find and 'amplify' positive deviance.

To do this, Sternin and his wife, Monique, knew that they

would have to help the Vietnamese find the answers to their needs in their own communities. The couple had just arrived in Vietnam and didn't know much about the country, including how poor parents could find food for their children, but they knew that a few people – the positive deviants – did. The trick was to find them.

So the Sternins, the Vietnamese Save the Children staff and a volunteer named Nguyen Thanh Hien brought villagers together to discuss solutions. What they eventually ended up with was a system for finding and promoting positive deviance:

1) Identify conventional wisdom

This is the way everyone usually does things. In Vietnam the conventional wisdom held that children with diarrhoea shouldn't be fed and that certain accessible types of food were too 'low class' to eat. In addition, mothers were failing to take an active role in making sure that their children got fed.

2) Identify the deviants

In this case, the deviants were those mothers whose children weren't malnourished. Their behaviours diverged from the conventional wisdom in numerous ways: they made sure that their children ate, even when they had diarrhoea, and they mixed their rice with sweet potato greens and tiny shrimp and crabs they collected from the rice paddies.

3) Encourage new behaviour

Sternin and Save the Children didn't tell the mothers they were working with what to do. They designed an intervention based on the deviant practices – in this case, getting small groups of mothers together to cook meals every day for two weeks, with each participant required to bring ingredients such as shrimp and sweet potato greens.

Each step in the process was carried out by the people whom this approach was meant to impact, so no one felt that they were being pressured to conform to practices brought in from abroad. The mothers in the pilot programme were trained to chart growth by age and weight, and after they had compiled a list of the children under the age of three in four villages, the Save the Children staff asked them if any poor families had well-nourished children. They saw for themselves that this was the case and they were eager to go back immediately to talk to the mothers to find out why.

The result: within two years, malnutrition had dropped 65 to 85 per cent in the villages Save the Children was working in and the changed behaviour was sustained. Children who hadn't even been born when the programme was launched were nourished at the improved levels.

The success, in short, was irrefutable. One reason they cited for their achievement was that they only brought in people who came from the same social and economic classes, so that they would see themselves as tackling shared problems with similar resources. 'You can't find someone whose uncle in the next village gives the family free medicine,' Sternin explains in the article: 'That solution won't work for everyone, because not everyone has such a resource.'[56]

It can be easiest to start off consultations with people who have a shared background. In some cases it's essential, particularly when people feel uncomfortable around individuals from other groups and when there's a history of antagonism or persecution between populations.

Ultimately, however, there's a limit to how much progress can be achieved when groups pursue solutions in isolation. Many of the world's seemingly intractable problems appear to be intractable precisely because people from different backgrounds keep themselves separated from each other. The rich uncle solution certainly isn't for everyone; but as the villagers learned when they discovered that the people eating 'low class' foods were healthier, sometimes solutions can come from unexpected places and expanding the range of people you're willing to learn from means increasing the odds that a solution that works for you can be found.

Considerations for Bahá'í Social and Economic Development Projects

Layli Miller-Muro is the founder and Executive Director of the Tahirih Justice Center, a Virginia-based non-profit organization established to provide legal representation and advocacy for immigrant and refugee women and girls facing gender-based violence. Something that's recently been on her mind is 'how Bahá'í a Bahá'í-inspired organization should be'.

For Bahá'ís who are wondering the same thing, she recommends asking some hard questions:

- How guided by Bahá'í principles do you want decision-making to be?
- Do you want Bahá'ís on your board of directors?
- Do you want Bahá'ís on your staff?[57]

Australia's Naveed Foundation funds projects that help to benefit the Bahá'í Faith as well as the larger community. In determining which projects to support, it relies heavily on the suggestions and advice of the National Spiritual Assemblies and Continental Counsellors of the areas that the projects serve.[58]

The Mona Foundation, on the other hand, explicitly states that it's not a Bahá'í organization. It is, however, guided by the principles outlined by the Office of Social and Economic Development at the Bahá'í World Centre and uses these principles to select its projects.[59]

At the Tahirih Justice Center, Miller-Muro had always assumed that most of the employees would be Bahá'ís. The opposite turned out to be the case: Bahá'ís comprise 40 per cent of the board of directors and three out of 12 of the staff members. Having people who aren't Bahá'ís running an organization that's based on Bahá'í principles can sometimes create interesting challenges. 'For example,' Miller-Muro explains, 'on our board, [officer] elections are conducted by secret ballot, which has to be explained and justified every year. The board's totally unfamiliar with that concept.'[60]

As it turns out, the non-Bahá'í board has made an effort to keep the Center aligned with its Bahá'í principles. To respect the fact that people of various faiths work at the Center, Miller-Muro had given the staff a lot of vacation time and told them to simply take off the holy days they observed. But the board of directors insisted that the Center should close on at least one Bahá'í holy day to make it clear that it was a Bahá'í-inspired organization. It also decided that the Center would not purchase alcohol for the events it sponsored.

The key to making this type of arrangement a success, Miller-Muro says, is to clearly define the organization's goals and outlook. 'They have to be defined,' she continues, 'because if not, you find yourself unconsciously going down a path that's on the whim of whoever happens to work at the organization at any given time.'

> If turning to spiritual values is a value of the organization, it has to be explicitly stated before people are hired . . . You've got to be transparent about your mission if you're guided by Bahá'í principles. A lot of people say they don't want to scare people but my experience is that telling people is not turning people off. They see it as an asset, not a liability. It's never hindered our opportunity to get funding. It's very, very common in the charitable field to have religious-inspired organizations. What frightens people is if they think you're hiding your agenda. Be clear about what you want, and state it.[61]

One of the ways the Tahirih Justice Center does this is by publishing a brochure that explains what being a Bahá'í-inspired organization means. 'For non-Bahá'ís, the brochure says what the Bahá'í Faith is, what being a Bahá'í-inspired organization means and doesn't mean. It doesn't mean we're trying to convert them. It does mean they might hear prayers.' For Bahá'ís, the brochure explains that the Center exists to provide a legal service, not – for example – to help Bahá'ís with their immigration problems.

Here's an example from Health for Humanity's policy guidelines:

In accord with clear guidance from [the Bahá'í Office of Social and Economic Development], HH is not involved in teaching the Bahá'í Faith . . . Individuals may share their beliefs privately as an outcome of their travel and/or services to others, but such teaching should be clearly segregated and detached from their services as members of HH. Mixing teaching of the Bahá'í Faith with HH health development efforts would jeopardize HH's grant funding, alienate donors, and invite opposition and criticism. HH does not have a 'hidden' agenda. Its sole purpose is to assist health development through a balanced approach using sound scientific methods together with universally accepted ethical principles . . . With this understanding, it is clear that all people, willing to conduct their activities in line with HH principles, are cherished in the membership rolls of HH. In fact, HH wishes to attract a more diverse membership and eagerly embraces all partners, regardless of race, religion, ethnicity, or gender.[62]

Culture

Miller-Muro points out that a Bahá'í-inspired organization has to ask itself about its culture: 'Do you observe Bahá'í holy days as a staff? Do you pray before staff meetings, even if most staff aren't Bahá'ís?'[63]

Fundraising

A Bahá'í-inspired organization should also ask itself questions about structure. For example, how will it raise money? Many charitable organizations raise money from the religious communities from which they emerge. In the United States, however, the National Spiritual Assembly has specifically asked organizations not to use Bahá'í membership lists to solicit funds.

An example of a specific fundraising question is whether or not to publicize donor names, such as on plaques or in newsletters. It's a common practice but as William Allmart, who runs the US Bahá'í Office of Development Research, points out, contributions to the Baháʼí Fund are anonymous. Should contributions to other organizations be different? 'Baháʼuʼlláh gave us these principles for a reason and one would think they should apply to every situation,' he says.[64] Currently, many Baháʼí-inspired organizations do publicize donor names.

Membership

Membership 'should be talked about from the beginning,' Miller-Muro states. 'Is being Baháʼí a criterion? It's OK as long as it's in the bylaws – Catholic Charities has in its bylaws that there's a quota of the number of Catholics who work there.' The Tahirih Justice Center never made being a Baháʼí a requirement for employment and it turned out that the overwhelming majority of qualified applicants for new positions were not Baháʼís.

Leadership

The Tahirih Justice Center has a highly unusual administrative component: a permanent board of directors that appoints the 'acting' board of directors but does not actually set policy or intervene in day-to-day operations.

'Most organizations just have a board of directors which elects itself,' Miller-Muro explains. 'The downside is this can become a political process. So Tahirih Justice Center has a "third layer" of permanent members, which doesn't change. All five of them are Baháʼís.' According to Miller-Muro, this de-politicizes the board of directors' work. 'The board still recommends its members, but it's a consultative process.'

At the Tahirih Justice Center, the permanent members do two things: appoint board members and approve changes to the articles of incorporation. The board of directors does everything else on its own, including modifying the organization's bylaws. 'It's a limited but safety net role,' says Miller-Muro. 'If something goes totally wrong, the permanent members could in theory fire the whole board. Traditionally, the board of directors perpetuates itself and there are some boards which have been taken over by dominant personalities who changed the mission of the organization.'[65] This type of structure is not possible everywhere.

Wally Verderoon, a member of Health for Humanity's board of directors, is a Lutheran. He doesn't think that acknowledging an organization as being inspired by Bahá'í or other principles 'is something we need to shy away from'. In terms of generating revenues and attracting talent, he points out, 'Notre Dame's connection to the Catholic Church has never seemed to affect it adversely.'[66]

6

Sustainability

Developing Human Resources

For projects to be sustainable, other people have to be trained to carry on our tasks after we've left. The community should never be made dependent on a particular person.

The teachers at Rabbani Bahá'í School believe that the purpose of development is not to do something for others but to train them to do it for themselves. Since one way to learn is by teaching, students become teachers. Standard 8(A) students (in the US, they'd be called eighth graders, about 13 years old) go to surrounding villages to teach the younger children there how to use rehydration salts for diarrhoea, while 8(B) students give training on the importance of immunization.

The Bahá'í International Community has stated that the primary task of development is to build capacity in individuals, communities and institutions to contribute to processes that will lead to a materially and spiritually prosperous society with fruits that can be enjoyed by all people.

Individuals can increase their capacities by coming to understand concepts, learn facts, master methods and develop the skills, attitudes and qualities necessary to lead a productive life.

Communities can build capacity by developing an environment that's conducive to the enrichment of culture.

Institutional structures can develop capacity by devolving decision-making to the lowest possible levels of the organization while facilitating cooperation and coordination on a large scale.

'Building the capacity of the peoples of the world and their institutions to participate effectively in weaving the fabric of a prosperous world civilization requires a vast increase in their access to knowledge,' the Bahá'í International Community asserts. This knowledge has two bases: the scientific method and the moral principles established by religion.[1]

The Badí' Foundation's programmes are designed to help participants change their own lives and make a positive impact in their communities. One of its initiatives is the Environmental Action Programme. Dr Noguchi explains:

> The Environmental Action Programme promotes understanding of sustainable development and action within a context relevant to the participants in the programme. The social enterprise projects and activities that arise depend on the needs and priorities of the participants themselves. For example, the Environmental Action Programme is used extensively with rural women and the women look at how to change their agricultural production systems to make them more sustainable. The first level course can be followed up with more specialized courses on different technologies, such as a production system including a biogas generator. When the Environmental Action Programme first level course is run with teachers, the emphasis is on environmental education. Teachers not only look at how to increase their students' knowledge about the environment but also how to involve their students in educating the greater community.[2]

The Rotary Foundation is interested in capacity-building through relationship development. Sabine Schuller, Programme Coordinator at the Rotary Foundation, which provides grants to Rotary clubs and districts, sees the development of relationships between these clubs and districts as an important part of the Foundation's work. 'From the staff's point of view,' she says,

> we measure the success of a project by confirming that the grant funds were spent on what the Trustees approved (e.g. the clubs

asked for money to build four bore wells, their report shows that they did indeed build four bore wells and they have pictures of happy villagers pumping water to prove it). We also look for active Rotary club participation. If one of the clubs did the majority of the work and as a result there was limited exchange of communication, relationship building, partnerships, we do not consider that project to be as successful as it could have been. It may be true that the four bore wells were built but if there was minimal contact/participation between the UK and Indian Rotary clubs, the staff believe a chance for relationship building and goodwill was lost.[3]

In the moral leadership model of development, people who want to improve their communities are encouraged to cultivate the capacities of the people around them. This means becoming acquainted with each person's capabilities with a view to inviting them to participate in tasks that they can learn from. It also means encouraging them to take initiative, even if we could have done the tasks more quickly ourselves.

Here, as in so many other places, moderation is key. Anello and Hernández advise that in our eagerness to train people, we shouldn't burden them with so many responsibilities that they become discouraged.[4]

Perseverance

The transformation of souls and communities can take time and requires patience.

One of the signs of a project's success, Dr Javid says, is simply survival under difficult circumstances. The fact that Ruaha has maintained its status as a school is, in and of itself, a success factor. For this reason, one of the criterion for projects that the Mona Foundation funds is that they have been in existence for at least three years.[5]

Big, splashy events have their place: they can inspire and motivate people and are used by many organizations to attract media attention. In Belize in 1992, Bahá'í youth held an event they called a 'Banner Run' – a day-long, 81-mile relay run from the country's western border with Guatemala to the Caribbean coast in the East. In front of the runner was a truck that held a large banner carrying Bahá'u'lláh's statement, 'So powerful is the light of unity that it can illuminate the whole earth.'[6] A group of ten or so youth at a time waited in the back of the truck for their turn to run. The rest of the youth rode in a bus behind the runner waiting to replace the ten youth in the truck.

The event was a huge success. It started off at dawn with a police escort in the border town of Benque Viejo, people came out to cheer the runners in the towns and villages they passed through and the mayor of Belize City gave a talk on the importance of race unity in the park where the runners ended up. The Bahá'í community of the western Belizean town of San Ignacio hosted the youth the night before the run and provided them with dinner and breakfast. The Bahá'í community of Belize's capital, Belmopan, met them in the middle of the day with lunch and the Bahá'í community of Belize City provided them with dinner in the park. The event was entirely planned by the Bahá'í National Youth Committee, which had only one member above the age of 21, and was covered by a newspaper, on television and on the radio. In short, it was incredibly successful in achieving its goal of raising awareness of race unity and demonstrating that a diverse group of people can realize major accomplishments by working together.

It did not, however, bring Belize's different cultures together permanently in a single day. That's a goal that requires perseverance on a vastly different scale than anything that can be achieved by one committee. On the other hand, even though it took place in the course of one day, preparing for the Banner Run itself was a long-term project. Planning started a year earlier. The process was made up of numerous small, measurable, concrete steps. Some people had to make the banner. Some people had to find the bus. Others had to coordinate the logistics to make sure that the runners would reach each stop on time or ask the mayor's office to participate. Not all of these steps got newspaper and television coverage. But they were still important.

How can people sustain their energy through such long-term operations? It helps to remember what you're working for and to keep your spirit refreshed. Professor Hanson suggests in her book *Social and Economic Development* that when people get mentally and physically tired, they can find sustenance by turning to prayer and reading sacred scripture.[7] Dr Anello and Ms Hernández write of the importance of transcendence, a vision of values and principles that have eternal worth. 'In this way,' they explain in *Moral Leadership*, 'it is possible to renew one's commitment in order to return to problematic situations with a broader perspective, a renewed vigour and a moral strength which enables the individual to carry on with his/her "work".'[8] This vision often comes from religion: in *The Secret of Divine Civilization*, 'Abdu'l-Bahá tells us that if Jesus' contemporaries had believed in Him, then 'through the quickening fragrance of His Spirit they would have regained their lost vitality and gone on to new victories'.[9]

Perseverance also becomes easier when we realize that we can't rely on any rewards beyond the action itself. Recognition is a great motivator. But it's not always going to be forthcoming. In His Farewell Address to the Letters of the Living, the Báb quoted words that He said had been spoken by Jesus to His own disciples: 'Such must be the degree of your detachment, that into whatever city you enter to proclaim and teach the Cause of God, you should in no wise expect either meat or reward from its people.'[10] Shoghi Effendi writes on the same theme: 'Let him not wait for any directions, or expect any special encouragement, from the elected representatives of his community, nor be deterred by any obstacles which his relatives, or fellow-citizens may be inclined to place in his path, nor mind the censure of his critics or enemies.'[11]

A long-term project is made up of many steps. The project should always be focused on its goal and should not be allowed to become an end in itself. Methods and their results must be evaluated, and if found lacking, adjustments must be made. Success depends on action, evaluation and adjustment.

Fellowship

People who are happy and get along with each other are more likely to be productive and stay together. As is the case in so many other areas, fellowship plays a big role in a project's sustainability.

One way to promote fellowship is to make sure that participants feel valued and respected. This means training with encouragement rather than criticism, letting go of the tendency to micro-manage others and giving people room to take ownership of the project – including the room to make mistakes in the course of their learning.

It also means showing people trust and being worthy of their trust oneself. In the words of 'Abdu'l-Bahá, 'Truthfulness is the foundation of all human virtues.'[12]

Nothing can cut short a promising project as quickly as back-biting. Once people start distrusting each other and spreading stories about their real or imagined shortcomings, communal projects become all but impossible.

In an infinite universe with infinite possibilities, it stands to reason that somewhere there's a place where nobody backbites. If you haven't found it yet, here are some suggestions for eradicating backbiting from the environment:

1) Make it clear that backbiting is harmful to the group and won't be tolerated. At the US Bahá'í National Center, staff members are told early on that backbiting isn't accepted.

2) Anecdotal evidence (in other words, I have no statistics to back this up) suggests that people are more likely to backbite when they feel powerless. Help people to feel empowered in their jobs, give them productive ways to express themselves and share their dissatisfactions as well as their praise. Make sure that the project is managed fairly and the chances that people will build resentment against each other will decrease.

3) Recognize that backbiting is sometimes associated with jealousy

and strive to create a social environment which workers perceive to be rational and fair.

Funding

The management of a long-term community development project requires sound business skills. Income and expenses will need to be projected. Planners will have to ask themselves how the project can be materially sustained.

For years the Albuquerque, New Mexico, Bahá'í community struggled to keep its weekly children's classes going. A few stellar teachers always rose to the occasion but there was never any consistency. Finally, the Local Spiritual Assembly set up a permanent school board with the task of hiring paid teachers and principals. The new Albuquerque Bahá'í School staff wasn't getting rich on its modest honorariums but the Assembly made its point: this was a serious project that was meant to last. The school wouldn't accept just any volunteers: all the teachers, principals and teachers' assistants would have to go through an interview process and agree to a regimen of periodic training before being accepted for the job. The honorariums were a sign of the community's commitment and a reminder of the important role that the teachers played. The result was that even after the teachers who founded the school and the first principal moved out of the area, the school continued to grow.

Those of us who are idealistic enough to want to start community development projects often don't want to tarnish our endeavours with anything so crass as the consideration of money. But this is a world in which spiritual principles are applied through material means. Basically, a secure source of funding can be crucial to a project's long-term success.

The question isn't just where material resources will come from in the first place. How will you generate money in the future? It's easy to get excited when a new project is starting and that's the time to figure out how to turn the initial enthusiasm into long-term strategies. After the Taliban were forced out of power in Afghanistan, the plight of the country's orphanages received widespread attention. One orphanage in Kabul received clothes, toys, even a soccer ball and a swing set. However, a year later most of the aid workers had left, the donations had stopped coming in and, according to an Associated Press report, 'little else has changed':

> Inside the cement-block building, dirt still cakes the grimy, unpainted walls. There is no heat in the dormitories, and in some rooms conditions are even worse than a year ago. Thin mattresses lie on the floor to accommodate the increasing number of children, who share dirty blankets and wrap themselves in ragged layers against the chill.[13]

Before we start an organization or a project, we should have an idea of how much it will cost to run. This will let us know the size of the grant we should ask for or how much funding we will need to raise from other sources.

When we're writing a grant proposal, we should make sure that all the costs are identified, well-defined and justified. Wally Verderoon has prepared a list of common expenses that organizations can use as a starting point:

Personnel salaries and benefits
Programme materials
Meeting expenses
Office supplies
Printing and photocopying
Postage
Computer equipment and software
Consulting services and honorariums
Telephone and other communications
Travel expenses
Food and beverages
Stipends for participants[14]

To which many organizations will have to add rent and utility bills.
At their simplest, our numbers will fall into two categories:

income and expenses. In other words, how much money can reasonably be expected to come in each month and from which sources? How much will be spent?

Within the category of expenses, there are two primary subcategories: fixed expenses and variable expenses. Fixed expenses remain the same every month: rent, for example, or utility bills. Variable expenses can change from month to month; for example, a one-time equipment purchase or a seasonal ad campaign to promote our services.

This overview can only approximate the complexities of an organization's accounting needs but provides a simple first way to sketch out its financial sustainability and helps us to determine how much we'll need to raise to accomplish our goals.

The Institute for Social and Economic Development (ISED) is a non-profit organization that works to strengthen the social and economic well-being of individuals and communities. The Institute notes that the techniques many middle-class people have used to amass enough assets to make them millionaires, as described in Thomas J. Stanley's book *The Millionaire Next Door*, can also be applied by non-profit organizations to reach financial stability. ISED lists five steps to attaining financial stability:

1) 'Quiet millionaires' establish financial goals. Organizations should establish financial targets, or benchmarks, to guide and help them measure their progress. The board of directors should set these goals and the executive director should execute them.

2) Millionaires buy a house as soon as possible. Organizations should buy the most valuable property they can afford and lease out excess space when the organization doesn't need it for itself. Paying a mortgage is an investment; paying rent is not.

3) Millionaires stay married to the same person. Organizations should invest in their staff members and strive to retain them. One way to do this is by developing a consensus about the organization's goals and the means of achieving them.

4) Millionaires save their money; organizations should establish a retained earnings or reserve fund goal.

5) Millionaires live frugally and organizations should too.[15]

There's another simple but crucial goal that should be at the top of every organization's financial agenda: diversifying funding sources. If most of an organization's revenues come from one or two places, it's at risk of going under as soon as one of those sources gets cut off.

The donor agencies that give grants are very well aware of this fact and they want to know that the recipients of their grants are thinking about it, too. If we're asking for a grant and we know of additional sources of funding, whether they've already committed money to us or we haven't even approached them yet, they should be mentioned in our grant proposal to let the grant-making foundation know that we're not relying on it for the entire success of our project.

Community development projects usually rely heavily on donations. The breakdown of Health for Humanity's budget for the fiscal year 2001 showed 81 per cent came from individual contributions, 13 per cent from business and corporate donors, 3.5 per cent from grants and 2.5 per cent from interest earned. Even more revenue was derived from non-cash contributions: the gifts it received in services, medical equipment and supplies, travel and facilities equalled two and a half times its entire cash budget.

Where do Health for Humanity's donations come from? Thirty-one per cent of its individual contributors are registered Health for Humanity members. The organization also holds two annual fund-raisers – a garage sale and a bowling/breakfast party – which rely on volunteers for inventory donations, set-up, sales and cooking duties. The breakfast generates income through entry fees, donations from people who were invited but couldn't attend, a silent auction, a raffle and sales of a 'Shirt-of-Fame' that features a list of donors' names.[16]

Fundraising will always present challenges and some of them

will be specific to certain locations and outlooks. For example, in the United States it's expected that non-profit organizations will aggressively fundraise. In Europe, asking for funds is much more likely to be considered inappropriate, although there are signs this is changing (some universities have hired American fund-raisers).[17]

Health for Humanity refuses to practice percentage-based fundraising. In other words, it doesn't give fund-raisers a percentage of the money they've brought in. Percentage-based fundraising has been associated with fraudulent activities so often that it's been banned by the Association of Fundraising Professionals, the Association of Healthcare Philanthropy, the Council for Advancement and Support of Education, and the American Association of Fund Raising Counsel.[18]

This is worth considering in more detail. After all, it's self-interest and the desire for profit that's supposedly at the foundation of the market system. 'We address ourselves not to their humanity, but to their self-love,' wrote Adam Smith of the market's actors.[19] So why would non-profit organizations have had problems with the extreme of this principle in practice?

'Abdu'l-Bahá indicated that business would inevitably evolve to include profit- and equity-sharing. These practices would be demanded by justice:

> No more trusts will remain in the future . . . Also, every factory that has ten thousand shares will give two thousand shares of these ten thousand to its employees and will write the shares in their names . . . and the rest will belong to the capitalists. Then at the end of the month or year whatever they may earn after the expenses and wages are paid, according to the number of shares, should be divided among both. In reality, so far great injustice has befallen the common people. Laws must be made because it is impossible for the labourers to be satisfied with the present system.[20]

However, justice isn't the only reason 'Abdu'l-Bahá gives. He also acknowledges profit as a legitimate motivator: 'For instance, the owners of properties, mines and factories should share their incomes with their employees and give a fairly certain percentage of their products to their workingmen in order that the employees may receive, beside their wages, some of the general income of the factory so that the employee may strive with his soul in the work.'[21]

In fact, when Bahá'u'lláh repealed Islam's prohibition on interest, the reason He gave was that interest drives commerce by providing an incentive for loans:

> As to thy question concerning interest and profit on gold and silver:.. Many people stand in need of this. Because if there were no prospect for gaining interest, the affairs of men would suffer collapse or dislocation. One can seldom find a person who would manifest such consideration towards his fellow-man, his countryman or towards his own brother and would show such tender solicitude for him as to be well-disposed to grant him a loan on benevolent terms . . . He hath now made interest on money lawful, even as He had made it unlawful in the past.[22]

There's nothing wrong with money. The problem is with our attachment to it. It's attachment, and not the money itself, that can distract us from our spiritual goals. This is true whether the money in question is ten dollars or a million. In Bahá'u'lláh's words: 'Disencumber yourselves of all attachment to this world and the vanities thereof . . . Know ye that by "the world" is meant your unawareness of Him Who is your Maker, and your absorption in aught else but Him.'[23]

The pursuit of profit, then, is appropriate so long as it's placed within the context of our broader objectives and doesn't become our purpose in itself. Vakil, for instance, in her 2001 essay about development for *The Journal of Bahá'í Studies,* concludes that the pursuit of profit can contribute to social and economic development if it's rooted in the struggle for human dignity.[24]

According to a position paper of the Association of Fundraising Professionals, the problem with percentage-based fundraising isn't with the seeking of personal profit. The problem arises from the fact that in order for an organization to maintain integrity, the people who work for it need to be motivated by the organization's goals. For a charitable organization, these goals are directed at service. The organization's integrity is also based on honest relationships with its donors, who freely contribute money with the understanding that it will be applied 'purposefully, effectively and efficiently' in support of the organization's mission.

By prioritizing a different set of values, percentage-based fundraising can set the stage for what the Association of Fundraising Professionals refers to as 'inappropriate conduct'.[25] Without spiritual and moral standards informed by a transcendent vision, we're inconstant. We're buffeted by the winds of every change of circumstance and susceptible to pressures placed by the people around us. On the other hand, for those whose foundation is permanent, 'the rain descended, and the floods came, and the winds blew and beat on that house; and it fell not: for it was founded upon a rock'.[26]

If you want someone to do great things, they need a great vision. When US Marines are sent into battle, they're not exhorted with promises of money. On the contrary, their missions are often presented in religious terms. As described in *The Atlantic Monthly*, they're inspired with 'a stark belief in their own righteousness, and in the iniquity of the enemy'.[27]

Many successful development projects, including Bahá'í-inspired initiatives, are funded by successful, for-profit businesses whose owners want to make a difference. Even if a project is conceived of as a stand-alone non-profit organization, in fact, it can still apply business strategies to its fundraising activities.

One example is the Hunger Site, a website that allows people to click on a link to provide free food to people in need. The funds

---

The Bible doesn't condemn money but it does condemn the love of money: 'For the love of money is a root of all *kinds of* evil, for which some have strayed from the faith in their greediness, and pierced themselves through with many sorrows.'[28]

for this seemingly simple project are generated through that most basic of business concepts, paid ads. After visitors click on the link, they're taken to a page of advertisements of companies that fund the site's altruism in exchange for the visitors' views.

The Hunger Site is also associated with an online store that gives a percentage of its profits to charity. The success of the Hunger Site has led to sister sites: the Breast Cancer Site (which funds free mammograms), the Child Health Site, the Rainforest Site (which pays for the purchase of rainforest land for preservation) and the Animal Rescue Site (which feeds animals in shelters). One of the benefits of the Hunger Site model is that it lets users take a simple action (clicking on a link) that makes them feel involved in the process.

The Internet should be part of our fundraising plans even if our core concept isn't Internet-based. There's no other medium that makes it so easy for people to contribute to projects immediately. The potential for non-profit organizations is enormous: one political action committee became a major force in American electoral politics after raising more than $2 million online for the 2000 US Congressional campaigns.[29]

If our organization is looking for money from individual contributors, it should consider giving them something small in return. Here's an interesting fact, which ties into our earlier consideration of profit and motives: many people want to be altruistic, but they're afraid that altruism isn't socially acceptable. What does this mean? They're willing to give more if they can make it look like they're acting out of self-interest. A study published in the *Journal of Experimental Social Psychology* found that when contributing to a charity that was important to them, people would donate three times as much when offered a gift but if they didn't support the charity's aims, the presence of the gift made no impact. In other words, they didn't care about the gift; they were just using it as an excuse to give a larger amount.[30]

Ultimately, a non-profit organization's ability to raise money will depend on its ability to inspire contributors with its vision. It should let supporters know exactly what their money is going to fund. One way to do this is to show them pictures of the people whose lives their gifts are helping. Another is to tell them stories of the impact the organization is making with their assistance.

Grants

Never tell a foundation that you need money. In the world of philanthropy, *need* is not a word to which people respond well. They want to be affiliated with winner organizations.

Successful organizations don't talk about their own needs, they talk about the ways that they can meet the needs of others. These organizations address two questions:

1) What are the needs of the community?
2) How have these needs been identified?

Question number two has a right answer. It is: 'Through the grassroots, from members of the community.'[31]

Verderoon provides some basic pointers for the pursuit of grant support. First, he makes it clear, we're not ready to go after grants until we've fully defined our goals and our strategies for measuring our progress against them. Once we've reached that point, we can begin looking for grant-making institutions with funding allocations that match our organization's objectives and projects.

Begin the search locally, Verderoon says, and then look in the indexes of the major foundation guides for grant categories that are compatible with your initiatives. Obtain the official grant application guidelines from the organization with a telephone call, a brief letter or by checking its website. When you're requesting a proposal, stick to the request. Don't say anything about yourself because at this point you might inadvertently tell them something which might disqualify you.

Read the grant application materials carefully. In fact, read them twice, to make sure you're not neglecting anything. Missing even a detail gives foundations an opportunity to throw your proposal away to make room for all the others crowding their desks.

Review the materials with your board of directors and determine if any of the staff, volunteer leaders or decision-makers at the foundation are connected to your board members in some way. If they are, they're potential contacts for the board members to pursue. (Board members should contact these decision-makers only after you've informed a programme staff member at the foundation about the contact in advance and after the initial formal approach is made to the organization according to its official application guidelines.) Develop, and set in writing, a strategy for interacting with the grant-maker.

Always contact a programme staff member at the grant-maker before submitting your proposal. If you send a grant proposal to a foundation where no one knows who you are, chances are good that they'll throw it away. (As should be clear by now, there are an awe-inspiring number of ways for your grant proposal to end up in the trash.) After the initial formal contact is made with the institution, usually through a letter of inquiry, speak to the programme staff member on the phone or in person. Determine the institution's current funding interests, share basic information on the project you're preparing the proposal for, ask for advice on how best to structure the proposal and set dates for the next steps or for the proposal submission. This is also the time to determine the general size of the grant your proposal will be targeting. 'Never leave the conversation without getting a number out,' Verderoon advises. 'Say what you're asking for, and set it higher than you want to see if you're in the right range.'

Finally, it's time to develop and submit the proposal based on the grant-maker's guidelines. 'Put language from the organization's guidelines in your proposal to show that you're addressing their needs and mission,' Verderoon counsels. Describe your project in terms of its relationship to your organization's mission, as well as to the foundation's interests. Very few organizations are unique, so on the very good chance that yours isn't, focus instead on what your organization does well. Formal grant proposals should be signed and submitted by your organization's chief executive officer.[32]

Soo-Jin Yoon is the evaluation officer of a grant-making institution in the southwestern United States. 'Our goal is to help the well-being of Coloradans and strengthen families,' she says, 'so all of our money goes into scanning Colorado's health issues and funding appropriate strategies within the state.'[33]

What is she evaluating? 'It's initiative-based grant-making: we don't just accept proposals, we design the initiatives. We send out the requests for proposals, people respond, and we select the grantees from that.' A method for evaluating the initiative is developed concurrently with the initiative itself. The purpose of the evaluation is to help Yoon and her institution gain a better understanding of how the initiative is actually working in the real world: whether it achieved the goals it was meant to achieve, for example, and the types of changes that were realized in the target population. 'I work alongside the programme officer in designing the evaluation,' Yoon says. 'Then we commission an evaluation firm to conduct it.'

In addition to an organization's past success rate, one of the criteria her institution uses to decide whether or not to award it a grant is how closely it addresses the questions in the request for proposals.

'It depends on the purpose of the initiative,' Yoon responds when asked to name other considerations that determine whether or not a grant will be awarded. 'There are a lot of different things that we all look at.' But there is one factor that can't be ignored: the likelihood that the organization will be able to pull off the project it's attempting. 'This can be kind of subjective,' Yoon acknowledges but there are certain variables which indicate a greater probability of project success. One of the big ones is whether or not the applicant has collaborators or partners, which are indicated by letters of agreement with other organizations.

Yoon's institution uses a standard scoring sheet to judge how well the project proposal matches the requirements set out in the request for proposals, which is usually very specific in terms of time frames and other project elements. 'You can't always tell just from the proposals what the grantee's going to be like, though,' Yoon says, 'because sometimes they just have a really good or poor grant writer, so we try to keep that in mind. Most of the people at the institution I work for have a lot of history in the community and know a lot of people, so the reputations and histories of organizations play a role. Our knowledge and experience with the grantees makes a difference.

'For some grantees, such as those working with immigrants and refugees, we wanted to make sure that we didn't just fund the big ones, but also funded grassroots organizations. We wanted to make sure to include a variety of capacities. We also try to fund urban and rural areas throughout the state, not just the metro Denver area.'

What mistakes do grant writers commonly make?

I would say the most glaring mistake is not addressing or responding to the request for proposals.

What characteristics do the best applications have?

They address the request for proposals but also show the organization's experience and show collaboration. A lot of times we fund community-based organizations, so it's really important for us to see that they have good collaborative relations with other organizations in the community. We also want to see their ability to address the issue at hand.

We also want innovative as well as evidence-based and model-based proposals.

More and more funders are looking for grantees to have evaluations, so there's a lot of pressure to have an evaluation component to their organization. It's not just us. Especially in light of the current economic situation, funders want to make sure their money is going to places where it will be used effectively. So evaluation is becoming more important.

I would also look for their ability to do the things they say they're going to do, and their capacities and past records.

What is the difference between a successful and unsuccessful organization when it comes to implementing projects?

There are certain elements that predict success, such as having strong and effective leadership.

We also provide a lot of technical assistance to the grantees, everything from board development to sustainability to leadership development, and they're more successful if they're conscious of those things.

Common mistakes are not having those elements. Grantees can also get so excited that they keep changing their plan and adding more things and becoming unrealistic in what they're trying to achieve.'[34]

If an organization hasn't received a response within two weeks of submitting its proposal, Verderoon suggests that it place a call to the programme officer to answer any of the institution's preliminary questions and find out when the grant decision date is, if it doesn't know it already. It should call again to check on the proposal's status after the decision date has passed. If the applicant receives significant good news about its organization or its projects before the decision is made, it can send the grant-making institution a brief letter announcing this fact.

Whatever the response ends up being, the applicant should send a letter of acknowledgement. If it didn't get the award, the letter should express gratitude for the opportunity and ask for advice about how to develop a more effective proposal in the future. The applicant should state that a follow-up call will be made by a leader at its organization and make sure the call takes place.[35]

Once an organization has received funds from a foundation, it should do its best to maintain a good relationship with it. In its July 2003 email newsletter, Vanguard Communications, a public relations firm, listed five ways that grantees could use communications to sustain their rapport with grant-making institutions.

1) *Be proactive*: Keep in touch with the organization informally throughout the year.

2) *Build relationships*: Connect with members of the organization as individuals and invite them to see where their money is going.

3) *Demonstrate sustainability*: Show the foundation that your organization will last even after their funding has stopped. Tell them about your long-term goals, highlight community partner-ships, profile individuals whose lives you've touched and display the response to your services.

4) *Practice transparency*: Report the results of your activities clearly and concisely. Be prepared to show financial information at any time. Use charts and graphs for clarification.

5) *Utilize Internet-based fundraising.*[36]

7

The Human Spirit

Transforming Souls

At its heart, community development isn't about building roads or donating computers. It's about transforming souls.

William E. Davis, then the Treasurer of the National Spiritual Assembly of the Bahá'ís of the United States and a founder and principal of a firm called DPK Consulting, spoke about one of the fundamental features of Bahá'í community development at the first North American Bahá'í Conference on Social and Economic Development in December 1993 in Orlando, Florida. Whereas traditionally development has been based on the delivery of services, Davis explained that Bahá'í development is based on the spiritual transformation of the individual and society and the cultivation of new patterns of interaction.

What does this mean? Every time we are part of a development activity, we should be asking ourselves how we can help people to come together and how much we are positively transforming souls.

The Bahá'í International Community stresses that 'it has become abundantly clear that materialist approaches alone will never succeed in releasing the power and building the capacity of individuals and communities to take action.'[1]

The application of Bahá'í principles to personal relationships can make an enormous difference to a community's prosperity. According to the World Bank, 'Studies show that societies where discrimination is greatest have more poverty, slower economic

growth and a lower quality of life than societies without discrimination . . . Educating girls is one of the most effective ways to
promote development.'[2]

It's worth noting that the most corrupt countries are also
the poorest. Corruption measurement is bound to be subjective
but one of the more comprehensive looks at the topic is Transparency International's Corruption Perceptions Index, which
combines data sources from multiple institutions, including the
World Economic Forum, the Economist Intelligence Unit,
PricewaterhouseCoopers and the World Bank. According to this
index, the most corrupt country in 2003 was Bangladesh, which
ranked 174 out of 208 in per capita income. Nine of the ten most
corrupt countries were among the poorest third in the world. (The
exception was Paraguay, the fourth most corrupt country but with
a relatively high per capita income ranking of 133.) On the other
end of the scale, Finland was the least corrupt country in 2003, and
ranked 13 in per capita income. The ten least corrupt countries were
all among the forty countries with the highest per capita incomes.[3]

Are countries corrupt because they are poor or poor because
they are corrupt? Evidence can be found for both arguments but
the fact is that poverty and corruption are often found together.

Gandhi always put personal transformation at the centre of
his own efforts. 'If one man gains spiritually,' he wrote, 'the whole
world gains with him, and, if one man falls, the whole world falls
to that extent.'[4]

On another occasion, Gandhi declared:

> Duties to the self, to the family, to the country and to the world
> are not independent of one another. One cannot do good to the
> country by injuring himself or his family. Similarly one cannot
> serve the country by injuring the world at large. In the final analy-
> sis we must die that the family may live, the family must die that
> the country may live and the country must die that the world may
> live. But only pure things can be offered in sacrifice. Therefore,
> self-purification is the first step. When the heart is pure, we at
> once realize what is our duty at every moment.[5]

Sustainable development, Mohan declares, is local and is based on individual empowerment. When people feel that they can make contributions to their surroundings, and put that feeling into action, they are initiating development. 'The people who help the sick people in their communities; the people who remember people's birthdays and make them feel special' are the true agents of change, he says. 'We tend to emphasize big projects, but community development is really about social transformation; people who touch other people's lives and change them forever. We have to focus not on large organizations but at the local level.' As an example, he points to the importance of the Bahá'í Feast that is held every 19 days. 'There are countless stories of people from warring tribes, different castes, coming together in 19 day Feasts.'[6]

Dr Sohayl Mohajer gives an example of transformation in action. 'One boy who came to Rabbani was always getting into trouble. But after a while his dad told me, "My son is trying to get me to do things differently. He tells me not to mix other metals with the gold I sell. I sent him to you to learn how to do things, not to become a priest." He withdrew his son from the school. But that is transformation. That is community development.'[7]

Dr Noguchi names character development as a primary goal of Macau's School of the Nations. 'The curriculum of the School of the Nations places significant emphasis on character development and service to others. The emphasis on character development is both a part of the formal curriculum and part of the overall atmosphere created at the school.'

What practical impact does this emphasis have? 'I think the programme really prepares students to be of service to their communities and to work together with others more effectively,' Dr Noguchi says. 'They are able to think more profoundly about the issues they will face as adults.'[8]

Quoting 'Abdu'l-Bahá, the Bahá'í International Community writes that 'Development, in the Bahá'í view, is an organic process in which "the spiritual is expressed and carried out in the material"'.[9]

'Communities that thrive and prosper in [the] future will do so because they acknowledge the spiritual dimension of human nature . . .' the BIC explains, and will remember 'that the interests of the individual and society are inseparable . . .'[10]

In fact, the BIC suggests that individuals and organizations pursuing social change devise spiritually-based benchmarks, or indicators, as bases on which to evaluate their programmes to make sure that they are incorporating the spiritual principles that are conducive to lasting development. The programmes could then adopt qualitative and quantitative measuring systems to determine whether or not these spiritual goals were being met. The BIC proposes five such indicators:

1) unity in diversity
2) equity and justice
3) equality of the sexes
4) trustworthiness and moral leadership
5) independent investigation of truth[11]

Unity in diversity means a global consciousness and a love of humanity as a whole coupled with an appreciation for different heritages, traditions and points of view. Equity means fairness and an equal access to resources and opportunities, while justice is the means by which fairness is applied. Equality of the sexes is necessary because when half of the population is suppressed, its ultimate progress is hampered. Trustworthiness within individuals, institutions, and communities is at the base of long-lasting and harmonious relationships. Moral leadership is leadership that is committed to social justice and service to humanity and commitment to a single standard of behaviour both for leaders and for other citizens. Independent investigation of truth implies a harmonizing of science and religion, an environment conducive to investigation, and an application of the principles of consultation.[12]

How might the application of these principles be evaluated? Here are some questions based on the principle of the independent investigation of truth that William E. Davis and Shahla Maghzi, a graduate student, posed in their analysis of a community-based natural resource decision-making process in Peru:

1) How clearly was the question under investigation framed both from a scientific and principled perspective?

2) To what extent did participants pool relevant information?

3) How common were face-to-face dialogues between technical experts, decision-makers and other participants?

4) How accessible and objective was information for all participants in the dialogue?

5) What was the extent of community participation in all phases of consultation and implementation?[13]

Professor Hanson stated at the 2000 Social and Economic Development Conference that the spiritual law of love can actually change the dynamics of economic systems:

Where many people still control their work – by producing crops on land they own, or producing crafts, or providing services – communities can consult together about how to ensure that their efforts are mutually beneficial. They can consider ways to enhance patterns of equitable exchange in the region. Where people are further removed from control of production and most of their economic activity is as consumers, they can still make their activity an expression of love by thinking about the human, social consequences of their economic actions.[14]

She presented these statements in the context of the words of 'Abdu'l-Bahá: 'When the love of God is established, everything else will be realized. This is the true foundation of all economics.'[15]

Human Nature

One of the many lessons of the 20th century was that no scheme, however clever, can succeed if it ignores human nature. The Soviet Union eventually disintegrated because its economy could not be sustained, and its economy could not be sustained because it contradicted human nature. For instance, Soviet citizens often did not feel that there was a connection between their actions and the results of their actions: some people would work hard without advancing, while others were able to manipulate the system for their own ends and give themselves benefits far out of proportion to their merits. Although these situations can be reliably used to describe much of human history, the communist system was practised in a way that consistently reminded people that their efforts did not matter. But as Bahá'u'lláh explained, 'That which traineth the world is Justice, for it is upheld by two pillars, reward and punishment.'[16] A successful system is one which allows people to be happy and fulfilled – in this example, by making them feel that their efforts can make a difference.

Art

Artists have an important role to play in development because they can inspire people and help them to see things in new ways. One way to help people reach their potential is to bring beauty into their lives, which is something that art can help to achieve.

'Art has the power to create change,' Mohan says. 'It's able to do that in a way that other things aren't. [Projects should be] commissioning and employing and utilizing artists because they're able to reach people's hearts.'[17]

Art can encourage people; it can also give them a new vision of the possible. Development that ignores peoples' drives and longings, that only engages them intellectually, will be harder to sustain. Art can awaken people's desire to work for social change and inspire their commitment to see it through.

Residents of the Korogocho settlement just outside of Nairobi,

Kenya, discovered the power of art first hand when a Chinese-born artist and activist named Lily Yeh started helping them use art to transform their environment. Korogocho is situated next to a huge city dump that attracts thousands of visitors each day who come looking for trash to recycle or subsist on.

Yeh first went to Korogocho at the end of 1993. For three months she collaborated with the local Paa Ya Paa Art Centre and a Catholic church to help residents beautify a courtyard by filling it with bright and colourfully painted angels and sculptures. She has continued to work with the community since then, finding local partners to help her teach residents how to use art to uplift their environments and their lives.

In the words of Elimo Njau, the director of Paa Ya Paa Art Centre, 'Lily Yeh's Korogocho Angel Project was like a radiant sunrise after a dark night, lighting up the worst slum in Nairobi with warm colours of great spiritual and material promise to the human spirit within the local community . . . This project brought dignity and pride to children and adults of Korogocho and elevated the human spirit above the pain and immense suffering of the over 100,000 people of the slum.'[18]

In chapter 2 we discussed the importance of people's mind sets on the lives they lead and the societies they help to create. Art both reflects and influences these mind sets. It helps us determine what the world looks like and where we fit into it. It tells us what is real and what is possible.

Consider the art historian Sister Wendy Beckett's description of painting's Northern Renaissance movement:

> The new form of painting that appeared in the Netherlands at the beginning of the 15th century was distinguished by a depth of pictorial reality that had not been seen before . . . the Flemish painters brought the sacred down to the real world. Instead of depicting a form of high drama for which the world served as a kind of grand stage, artists chose to portray real-life domestic interiors . . . We find a growing peace with the world and one's place in it . . .[19]

We see the same interaction between art and a changing way of looking at the world in her introduction to the French Romantics:

> While Neoclassicism was associated with the culture of antiquity, the Romantic was associated with the modern world . . . The necessary strategy for such expression was inevitably incompatible with the dogma of Neoclassicism and its established boundaries of beauty and subject matter . . . Romanticism stands for an outlook, an approach, a sensibility toward modern life.[20]

Art can also awaken within us an appreciation of our higher natures and become a means by which our souls 'may be lifted up unto the realm on high',[21] as Bahá'u'lláh says of music.

Hope

The Universal House of Justice, in a letter written in 2003 to the Bahá'ís of Iran, noted that the way people are treated, particularly systematic oppression, can impact their view of themselves and their ability to act positively on their own behalf:

> Deliberate oppression aims at dehumanizing those whom it subjugates and at de-legitimizing them as members of society, entitled to neither rights nor consideration. Where such conditions persist over any length of time, many of those affected lose confidence in their own perceptions of themselves. Inexorably, they become drained of that spirit of initiative that is integral to human nature and are reduced to the level of objects to be dealt with as their rulers decide. Indeed, some who are exposed to sustained oppression can become so conditioned to a culture of brutalization that they, in their turn, are ready to commit violence to others, should the opportunity offer itself.[22]

The Universal House of Justice goes on to observe that although the Bahá'ís of Iran suffered persecution that was designed to produce these results, they instead responded with magnanimity, love and the acquisition of spiritual qualities and mental development. Why? Their religious faith.

As the former Director of the US Bahá'í Refugee Office, Puran Stevens has seen her share of suffering. Whether in refugee camps in Thailand and the Philippines or in interviews with victims of imprisonment, torture and exploitation who have sought asylum in the United States, she's seen first hand how much pain one human can inflict on another and how much the human spirit can endure. She's also seen how successful people can be when they have a vision: the Iranian Bahá'ís in the United States, for example, many of whom entered the country as refugees or immigrants and who together only comprise about 13 per cent of the American Bahá'í community, contribute an estimated 44 per cent of its volunteer service and financial resources.

According to Stevens, what people most need in order to survive and excel is hope. If you want to make a difference, she says, if you want to change someone's life, give him hope. Become a mentor to someone; befriend him and visit him; let him know how much potential he has.

Love

At the Church of the Ascension in New York, 'Abdu'l-Bahá was asked whether peace was a greater word than love. He responded:

> No! Love is greater than peace, for peace is founded upon love. Love is the objective point of peace, and peace is an outcome of love. Until love is attained, peace cannot be; but there is a so-called peace without love. The love which is from God is the fundamental. This love is the object of all human attainment, the radiance of heaven, the light of man.[23]

Numerous studies have shown that children who are raised in conditions of economic hardship are more likely to exhibit signs of behavioural problems and decreased intelligence. According to a study of 1,116 mothers and their five-year-old same-sex twins in poor households in England and Wales published in the May 2004 issue of *Child Development*, children could 'rise above' extreme poverty and the conditions associated with it, such as homes that were damp, overcrowded or dilapidated, if they received love from their parents – specifically, 'warmth, mental stimulation and interest'. Along with genetics, which was an important but not the only factor in the children's success (genes explained 70 per cent of the variability in children's behavioural resilience and 46 per cent of the difference in their cognitive ability), how the mothers treated their children played a major role in their children's cognitive development and behaviour. Only mothers were studied because most of the children in the poor neighbourhoods where the research was conducted grew up in single-parent homes.[24]

Love is the key to harmonious social interaction and individual transformation. In chapter 3 we considered the idea that love is expressed individually through mercy and collectively through justice. Ultimately, this means that when we strive for justice, we're working to infuse love into our social affairs.

If we really want to make the world a better place, we need to treat each other with love and affection. As Hillel said of the golden rule, that is the entire law; 'Everything else is commentary.'

8

Reflections on Positive Change

I am optimistic about the future. I have faith in divine guidance, and never cease to be impressed with human compassion and ingenuity. But certain numbers are hard to ignore. One of them is 32. That's how many more times the resources I consume – if I am an average westerner – than an average person who lives in the developing world. It's also the number of times more trash and waste I leave.[1] Meanwhile, 420 million people live in countries that no longer have enough cropland to grow their own food, and more than half a billion people live in water-poor regions that are prone to chronic drought.[2] If everyone on the planet woke up tomorrow with the standard of living that we now equate with the developed world, how would we sustain it?

Over the course of the past seven chapters, we've looked at practical ways to initiate and sustain social change at increasing levels of complexity. The emphasis has been on social and economic development. As we've discussed, however, development means more than simply transferring resources, or even raising standards of living, although both of these goals are essential. Sustainable development requires mental revolutions and spiritual transformations. We need to find new ways of dealing with the problems that confront us.

The tools we use to resolve our challenges are based on our vision of the world and our place within it. For that reason, this last chapter will be less about specific tools, as some of the earlier chapters were, and more about how we may approach contemporary problems in general. We'll start off with a look at the connection between justice and an independent investigation of the truth, move next to the importance of expanding our circles of fellowship, and end with a vision of human rights that is grounded in a spiritual concept of humanity.

This chapter isn't intended to be a conclusion. Hopefully, it will serve instead as a bridge to further reflection and momentum on the path of positive social action.

Justice and Investigation

The pursuit of justice requires an investigative approach to the world. In order to act justly, individuals and institutions need to reject prejudice and try to understand the facts of the situations that face them. Prejudice gets in the way of justice, and independent investigation gets in the way of prejudice. In the words of Bahá'u'lláh:

> The best beloved of all things in My sight is Justice; turn not away therefrom if thou desirest Me, and neglect it not that I may confide in thee. By its aid thou shalt see with thine own eyes and not through the eyes of others, and shalt know of thine own knowledge and not through the knowledge of thy neighbour.[3]

Bahá'u'lláh also addresses this theme in the Tablet 'Words of Wisdom'. 'The essence of all that We have revealed for thee is Justice, is for man to free himself from idle fancy and imitation, discern with the eye of oneness His glorious handiwork, and look into all things with a searching eye.'[4]

Investigation leads to knowledge and is in consequence a tool of empowerment. Rulers have inevitably tried to retain control of unjust systems by keeping knowledge away from others. In the Kitáb-i-Íqán, Bahá'u'lláh discusses oppression by 'foolish leaders' who place their own ambition over an impartial search for knowledge: 'With all their power and strength they strive to secure themselves in their petty pursuits, fearful lest the least discredit undermine their authority or blemish the display of their magnificence.'[5]

Such rulers recognize knowledge as a key to social action. Through its acquisition, people come to understand the conditions they live in and how to improve them.

There are many forces that affect our willingness and ability to investigate the issues that affect us, and they range from the external, such as control of access to information and the politicization of knowledge, to the internal, such as the lie of silent assertion and wishful thinking. We'll consider these four forces below, and then we'll look at solutions.

1) Control of access to information

It's not surprising that when one group wants to keep another under control, it almost invariably tries to manipulate that group's access to information. It might also try to keep information away from the people who want to help them. In Sudan, by the beginning of July 2004, a 16-month conflict had led to between 10,000 and 30,000 deaths, and up to one million people had been driven from their homes. A Sudanese newspaper commenting on this tragedy printed the intentionally misleading headlines 'Situation in Darfur Under Control' and 'Ethnic Cleansing Sheer Fabrication'. When UN Secretary General Kofi Annan flew into Sudan to talk to refugees about the situation they faced, a refugee camp he was planning to visit, holding 3,000 to 4,000 people, was emptied by the government before his arrival. Officials explained that the refugees had been moved for their own good.[6]

2) Scientific data as a political tool

Even scientific data, which is ostensibly objective, can be used as a tool of political expediency. During the same month that Annan went to Sudan, July 2004, the US federal government and the state of California were engaged in a dispute about whether or not carbon dioxide was a pollutant. California said that carbon dioxide emissions from vehicles were contributing to global warming and wanted cars sold in the state to be redesigned to be more fuel efficient. The federal government asserted that carbon dioxide couldn't be an air pollutant because it's nontoxic and found in nature, and therefore its emission shouldn't be regulated. Both claims were technically sound; both also coincided exactly with each government's respective positions on whether or not car manufacturers should be required to increase gas mileage.[7]

3) The lie of silent assertion

It's not always easy for us to investigate reality for ourselves when everyone around us is repeating a popular prejudice. Mark Twain coined a term, 'the lie of silent assertion', for a population's willingness to buy into falsehoods by simply acceding to the accepted truths of the day.

> For instance. It would not be possible for a human and intelligent person to invent a rational excuse for slavery; yet you will remember that in the early days of the emancipation agitation in the North the agitators got but small help or countenance from anyone. Argue and plead and pray as they might, they could not break the universal stillness that reigned, from pulpit and press all the way down to the bottom of society – the clammy stillness created and maintained by the lie of silent assertion – the silent assertion that there wasn't anything going on in which humane and intelligent people were interested.[8]

4) Wishful thinking

We're often among the first victims of our own unreliability, especially when it comes to wishful thinking. Think of the American Internet stock bubble in the late 1990s: companies that wanted to cash in but hadn't yet developed a sound business plan told investors that in the new economy, what mattered in the short term was not how much money they made ('the stocks' price to earnings ratio') but how much attention they managed to win for themselves ('brand saturation' – you had to use the right terms to make it sound believable). In other words, the more money they spent, the better, just as long as their flashy expenditures got people's attention. In the long run, once everyone knew who they were, they could concentrate on the money-making aspects of their businesses, assuming they had developed those aspects by then.

There was no evidence to suggest that this approach would be successful, and it flew in the face of everything that companies had been learning about sound management over the previous century.[9] But investors lined up to give them money because they wanted to cash in, too. Although at the time its waste was frustrating, in retrospect it's hard not to feel awe at the sheer audacity of a company like Pixelon, which spent $12 million of the $30 million it had raised on its launch party.

Wishful thinking is hard to overcome, and the phenomenon had no problems surviving the crash that wiped out the Pixelons of the day. It just took different forms. One hoax promising its users money from Microsoft founder Bill Gates if they forwarded it on to friends was started in 1997 by a college student as a joke, and its propagation showed no signs of slowing by 2004.[10]

Fortunately, just as there are many factors that can erode our ability or willingness to investigate the truth, there are many tools and principles that can help us to view the world with a just and searching eye. To give four examples, we can give a prominent place in our thinking to verifiable facts, promote education, ask questions and avoid dogmatism.

a. Collect facts

Niccolò Machiavelli's *The Prince* has been inspiring and guiding political leaders since the early 16th century. The basic premise of *The Prince* is generally held to be that the end justifies the means, and by this late chapter it's hopefully clear that this approach leaves something to be desired. However, I believe that there's another reason why Machiavelli has made such an enduring impact on so many generations of leaders, those people who have wanted practical advice for gaining power and effecting change: *The Prince*'s particulars might focus on Renaissance politics, but in general it's about the importance of evaluating a given situation and potential responses based on what it is, rather than what people have generally claimed it to be. The irony of Machiavelli's legacy is that he apparently penned *The Prince* in the wishful but mistaken belief that it would secure him a position under the de Medicis, when his own political ideal was not a principality but a republic.

b. and c. Promote education and ask questions

Education empowers people and gives them the tools to advance themselves and the world around them. So does access to information. There is a simple methodology that can help people to gain education, evaluate their environments and avoid being manipulated by groups with obscure agendas: asking questions. 'Questions' is such an important concept for the current stage of humankind's development that it's the name of the one of the Bahá'í months.

d. Avoid dogmatism

Being open to knowledge means avoiding dogmatism. An instructive lesson in this regard can be gained from the Universal House of Justice, the supreme administrative body of the Bahá'í world. Organizations always seem to want to produce issue statements on new topics as soon as they're introduced – but not so the Universal House of Justice. Asked in 1998 about cloning, the Universal House of Justice indicated that research was at an early stage, nothing specific had been found in the Bahá'í writings on the topic, the Universal House of Justice considered it premature to give consideration to the matter then, and Bahá'ís could come to their own conclusions based on their study of the Bahá'í writings and their own consciences. They should also avoid making dogmatic statements on the topic. Questions about genetic engineering and stem cell research received similar responses.[11]

On another occasion the Universal House of Justice wrote, through its Secretariat:

This is the age in which mankind must attain maturity, and one aspect of this is the assumption by individuals of the responsibility for deciding, with the assistance of consultation, their own course of action in areas which are left open by the law of God . . . It should also be noted that it is neither possible nor desirable for the Universal House of Justice to set forth a set of rules covering every situation . . . In such aspects of morality, the guidance that Bahá'í institutions offer to mankind does not comprise a series of specific answers to these moral issues, but rather the illumination of an entirely new way of life through the renewal of spiritual values.[12]

Progress is most likely in an environment where trust is cultivated and the pursuit of knowledge is prized. In the model of moral leadership defined by Dr Anello and Ms Hernández, agents of social change are encouraged to concern themselves with two categories of truth: the 'contingent truth', or the facts about how things are; and the 'ideal truth', which is a vision of how things should be. The former requires investigating the world and its conditions; the latter means employing the tools of religion. The ultimate ideal truth is that divine standard proclaimed by God's revelators. 'If you abide in My word, you are My disciples indeed,' Jesus said to the Jews who believed in Him; 'And you shall know the truth, and the truth shall make you free.'[13]

In order to ascertain ideal truth, we have to free ourselves of our learned prejudices. Once we have knowledge of these two categories of truth, we are in a position to establish a process for transforming the contingent truth into the ideal.[14]

Challenging Injustice: Protest and Globalization

Positive social change has often begun with protest, but it doesn't end there. Injustice should never be left unchallenged. Bahá'u'lláh calls on each of His followers to be 'an upholder and defender of the victim of oppression'.[15] But lasting change doesn't just come from condemning something; it comes from people's ability to find and take advantage of alternatives. As agents of change we should be encouraging anything that cultivates understanding and reflection and helps people to come together to share information through dialogue.

In the United States protest has had a successful and justifiably proud history. The 1963 March on Washington, led by Martin Luther King, Jr., was a crucial rallying point in the evolution of US social consciousness, an event that forced Americans to confront their country's institutionalized racism. This is what protest is best at: bringing to light an issue that many people care about but feel that individuals or groups in positions of authority have ignored.

Unfortunately, protest also has a tendency to create false dichotomies. It's very difficult to protest in a way that engages people in an open consultation and allows them to figure out what something actually means and how to productively address it.

Globalization, one of the most prominent targets of modern protests, can serve as a useful example. I was introduced to anti-globalization movements in 1995. In the Indian state of Karnataka, I went to the first KFC restaurant to set up shop in the capital city of Bangalore. The glass doors were protected by a sliding metal gate, which was kept half-closed during business hours. Just outside of the doors two members of the Bangalore police force stood guard, casting watchful eyes over the street. At the end of the block was a police van with ten additional officers, alert for any signs of trouble. These were the reasons I had come to the restaurant, contradicting my usual stance that there's no adventure in dining on American food in a foreign country.

Why was the Colonel's eatery such an exciting place? The Karnataka Farmer's Association had threatened to blow it up. It claimed that the foreign fast food was unhealthy, that the restaurant did not use Karnataka-raised chickens and, most importantly, that allowing its parent company, Pepsi Foods, to make inroads into the Indian economy was a surrender to economic imperialism and a prelude to potential slavery to the West. On the other hand, the government wanted the money and enough Bangalore citizens wanted the food for the company to set up shop. Pepsi, the Karnataka farmer, and the government of Karnataka were caught in the middle of the question of whether multinational corporations' harm outweighs their help, or the other way around.

Divorced of the social and regulatory trappings of the countries in which they emerged, western products transplanted into foreign soil arrive accompanied with a lot of greed and only a little responsibility. Multinational corporations' wealth and power often make local governments dependent on them. They drive local firms out of business and become monoliths in local economies. In the 1970s, six multinational corporations controlled 70 per cent of world aluminum production capacity and three multinational corporations controlled 70 per cent of the world's production, marketing and distribution of bananas. Multinational corporations also often borrow from local capital, already scarce, rather than bring in new funds because local banks are likely to give them preferential treatment owing to their size and resources. They also enter many countries by taking over existing businesses and then driving competitors out of business, which does little to encourage local entrepreneurship. Through transfer pricing, subsidiaries of a multinational corporation exchange goods to show less profit in developing countries where many products are assembled and more profit in developed countries which have lower taxes, thus enabling them to avoid often higher taxes in the developing countries and ultimately keeping more of their money from entering the local market. (When a multinational corporation doesn't do this, it is often enjoying large tax breaks as a perk for operating in the developing country.) And a lot of the profits are simply repatriated to shareholders in the corporation's country of origin.[16]

The environment is another casualty of the strength of multinational corporations. Mexico's environmental protection laws are much softer than those of the US and, throughout the 1980s, the 1,800 US-owned product assembly plants on the Mexican side of the US-Mexican border took full advantage of that discrepancy. Many of them had relocated to Mexico, in fact, for that precise reason. The American National Toxic Campaign surveyed 23 of these factories and found that 17 were responsible for major toxic waste discharges. And most of Southern California's furniture industry moved south of the border to escape California's strong air pollution controls on solvent emissions.

These are all glaring arguments against multinational corporations. There are also counter-arguments in favour of their international impact: they can help the economies of developing countries through the infusion of capital, technology and management expertise and through their access to developed marketing networks.

The reason why protesting globalization is counterproductive, however, isn't because of this infusion of capital and expertise. It's because of the very reasons which make multinational corporations potentially dangerous. America's biggest corporations are wealthier and more powerful than almost every country they do business in. Wal-Mart makes more money in a year than the gross domestic product of Austria, Turkey or Norway. Exxon Mobil has more money than Ireland, New Zealand or Egypt. General Motors has a bigger income than the gross domestic product of Malaysia, Thailand or Greece. The only way smaller countries can keep from being exploited is if there are international standards for the way businesses behave. In other words, the solution to these problems is globalization.

People in developing countries want jobs. They want the goods and services which those jobs help them to purchase. Globalization can't be stopped. It can, however, be improved. If the forces contributing to globalization were harnessed for promoting universal human rights and global environmental protection standards, then firms could not flee these norms by going to other countries, workers in developed countries would not have to worry that the reason for their job losses was that people in other places were labouring in dangerous conditions for terrible pay, and there would be fewer people in developing countries being taken advantage of, which are the common, and well-founded, concerns of many in the anti-globalization movement.

The irony is that anti-globalists and the institutions they protest often claim to want the same things. In 2000, while protestors in Washington DC marched in protest of meetings of the World Bank and the International Monetary Fund, the president of the World Bank sighed during an interview and said, 'They [the protestors] could be quoting from what I've been saying for the last five years.'[17]

Naomi Klein, the author of *No Logo*, a book that looks at some of the more disturbing practices of corporate globalization, argues in her analysis of post-war Iraq that it is only international law – specifically, the Geneva Conventions of 1949 and the Hague Regulations of 1907, which prevent occupying powers from stripping resources from the countries they control – that stopped Iraq's resources from being completely handed over to foreign companies in 2003.[18]

As for India, since it started engaging in the global economy it has developed many new white-collar jobs – more than 300,000 in 2004. A lot of those jobs have gone to Bangalore.[19]

The problems created by the emergence of a global community that has not yet established a means of global decision-making and problem-solving require global solutions that take into account the oneness of humanity, and more, not less, information-sharing and consultation. It's no longer enough to say we don't like something; it's time to cultivate an environment that is conducive to the investigation of alternatives.

Working Together

Back in chapter 1 we considered the importance of transcending partisanship. The fundamental danger of partisanship is that it prompts a willingness to sacrifice the greater good for parochial or individual goals. It's based on the erroneous conclusion that it's somehow possible for the part to prosper while the whole it's a part of declines.

There's another model for social action. It involves building something positive rather than just attacking something negative. This is not an easy thing. It's an act of faith and confidence.

Partisanship can arise from noble aspirations, such as a commitment to one's immediate group and a legitimate concern about the relative merits of innovation and tradition. Both of these motivations find expression in the protests of people around the world who are afraid that accepting progress means allowing alien values to be imposed on them from outside.

Let's use the writings of an Arab thinker named Adil Hussein as an example. Hussein wrote that the Swedish economist Gunnar 'Myrdal – and naturally others' – explanations of modernization values are confined to rationalism, development planning, higher productivity, institutions, proper policies and the like. Yet the list of values does not include the most important one necessary for development, which is self-confidence in dealing with dominant and domineering foreign influences.'

To Hussein, self-confidence meant turning to one's nation for development and rejecting foreign ideas of advancement. 'The Ottomans established a number of schools in the new style and sent their youth to Western countries to bring back with them the science, knowledge, literature and all that they call "civilization". Yet this civilization is directly related to its country of origin, and in accordance with the nature and social structure of that country and its people.' He acknowledged that different nations and cultures interact but his very definition of a nation was a people for whom 'all their cultural achievements (of all types and forms) were original, not drawn from outside'.[20]

Is this the only route to cultural preservation? Do we have to choose between global homogeneity and retreating to parochial fortresses that reject 'science, knowledge, literature and all that they call "civilization"'? Or is it possible to appreciate and even retain diversity while allowing our own and other nations to advance? I believe that it is.

S. Nagaratnam, a member of the Continental Board of Counsellors (an appointed Bahá'í institution with an advisory and consultative role) for Asia, addressed the concern at the heart of the retreat that Hussein describes in a film about Indian Bahá'ís called *The Heart of the Lotus*. Nagaratnam pointed out that in the past, when people recognized the need for change, they often destroyed what they had previously believed in, the good along with the bad. By contrast, he said, one of the things the Bahá'í Faith taught people in India to do was to work for change by adding whatever was necessary for a new age while retaining whatever was positive from their past.[21]

In *The Secret of Divine Civilization*, 'Abdu'l-Bahá responds to the charge that it's unpatriotic for one culture to borrow from another and demonstrates that the West itself reached its material prominence by borrowing from Islam. For example, Europeans took the idea of the compass from the Arabs and used it to navigate around the world.

Sociologists have given a lot of thought to the reasons why cultures are often able to do more with advances borrowed from other cultures than those which are developed indigenously. In the United States, for instance, American car makers were shocked in 1979 to discover that Japanese manufacturers had claimed over a fifth of the domestic auto market. One suggestion is that in their countries of origin, innovations become linked to particular traditions and mental models which define and limit their uses. When they are exported to other cultures that lack those traditions and models, they can be applied in new ways.

What's clear is that whatever increases people's ability to connect with each other, whether that connection is based on technology, a shared language or the recognition of our common humanity, can lead directly to improved standards of living. That's a point well understood by the one in eleven Africans who are now cell phone users. Farmers use the cell phones to improve their negotiations by learning prevailing crop prices, and rural healthcare workers use the phones to summon ambulances.[22] In his book *The Lexus and the Olive Tree*, journalist Thomas Friedman quotes a former investment banker turned socially conscious entrepreneur who explains simply: 'Connectivity is productivity, be it in a modern office or an underdeveloped village; connection enables, disconnection disables.'[23]

Our ability to reach out to other people contributes to development. It also contributes to justice.

Time and again, people who have claimed to fight for justice have ultimately refused to extend their ideas about justice to groups that for one reason or another they didn't identify with. In other words, they abandoned their ideals for the sake of factionalism and partisanship. The 20th century featured one revolution after another in which the revolutionaries ended up turning into the type of autocrats they had started out trying to fight. The major difference was that now their group was in control instead of another group. And often a third group, oppressed by the second group, would begin its own rebellion and the process would begin again.

When Hania Mufti, a researcher for Amnesty International, entered Kuwait after the occupying Iraqi soldiers were driven out in the Gulf War, she discovered that Kuwaitis were carrying out widespread acts of vengeance against perceived collaborators, mostly foreigners. As the writer William Langewiesche explained in *The Atlantic Monthly*, 'This particular pattern – of the oppressed becoming the oppressors when the tables suddenly turn – is a perpetual problem for human-rights activists, and an indication of the structural challenges that they face in their attempt to remake human behaviour.'[24]

When people say they're fighting for justice, what they often mean is that they're fighting for an end to their own group's oppression. Lasting change requires people who are willing to fight against oppression itself. To fight, not against a group, but for a system in which all groups are able to work together.

The Nazi party of Germany and the Communist party of the Soviet Union repeatedly justified their own rise to power by pointing out the evils of the other. The Nazis made anti-Communism part of their campaign platform, and the Soviets were staunch anti-Nazis who helped to defeat the Third Reich during World War II. Both parties ended up as authoritarian regimes that executed their own people in droves. At the height of the cold war, the United States adopted authoritarian techniques, in the form of Senator McCarthy's Un-American Activities hearings, in an attempt to oppose Soviet authoritarianism.

In the Christian world, the Pope of Rome and the Patriarch of Constantinople found it impossible to cooperate even though they ostensibly belonged to the same religion and were thus unable to defend themselves as much of eastern Christendom fell to Islam. In the 15th century, with Constantinople and the rest of eastern

Christendom threatened by the Turks, the Western and Eastern Churches tried to hammer out an agreement that would allow them to support each other. One of their primary disputes was over whether the Holy Spirit proceeded from both the Father and the Son or just from the Father. (The Patriarch of Constantinople and his Emperor insisted on the latter.) Pope Eugene IV commissioned a fleet of ships to bring the eastern Emperor and the Patriarch first to Ferrara and then to Florence in 1438, in which city a 'Decree of Union' was finally settled. In the end, though, the leaders of the Eastern (or Byzantine) Empire found the compromise too much to swallow, even after 1453, when their empire fell to Turkish forces. As the *Encyclopedia Britannica* describes this rift, which still divides Christianity, 'the orthodox Greek nationalists feared Latinization [by Rome] more than Mahommedan rule'.[25]

On the other hand, Islam became the most advanced civilization in the world thanks in large part to its willingness to embrace ideas different from its own. It's easy now to forget that Islam once led the world in knowledge but in *Story of the Church*, a history textbook written in 1935 by two priests and a nun for Catholic schoolchildren, the authors freely admit that the Muslims' 'knowledge of philosophy and the sciences seemed very impressive to many Christians with whom they came in contact, and these, as a consequence, came to doubt their own religion'.[26]

Islam achieved its position of intellectual eminence not only because of its veneration of the written word, which was reinforced by the cultural prominence of the Qur'án, but also because its adherents translated Greek and Roman philosophy into Arabic and elaborated on ideas from other cultures, including Hinduism (such as the zero, which helped the Muslims develop algebra). Although Christians and Jews were second-class citizens in Muslim lands, they were usually protected and sometimes flourished. Eastern Orthodox, Syrian Orthodox, Coptic and Nestorian Christians were among the churches that thrived under Islamic rule while being condemned, and in many cases hunted down and killed, by the Catholic hierarchy in Europe. And Catholics fared well under Muslim rule, too. When Christians re-conquered

Spain, the Jews there fled – many of them to Muslim territories. All these groups enriched Muslim civilization.

The Muslims' tolerance can be traced back to Muhammad, who, when He conquered Mecca, called it a 'day of mercy', refused to harm anyone in the city who had led attacks against Him and left all the pictures of Jesus and Mary in the Ka'bih intact. Muhammad's Charter of Privileges to the monks of the St Catherine Monastery on Mt Sinai declared, 'Christians are my citizens; and by God! I hold out against anything that displeases them.' Their property and churches were not to be disturbed, their monks should remain in their monasteries and Christian women could not be married to Muslim men without the women's permission, in which case they should be allowed to visit their churches to pray. 'No compulsion is to be on them,' the Charter stated. ' . . . No one is to force them to travel or to oblige them to fight. The Muslims are to fight for them.'[27]

Muslims benefited from the tolerance they showed to the Christians and Jews, and Jews benefited from their willingness to work with the Muslims. As soon as the Muslims conquered the Persian Empire, they restored wealth and power to the Jewish leaders there and created an atmosphere in which the great Jewish academies of Babylonia could be reopened, leading to a renaissance of Jewish thought which exerted its influence for centuries.[28]

Communities that attack each other because they have different ideas undermine their own strength. Communities that work together despite their differences prosper.

The struggle for justice is not a fight against some particular group, some political party or nation or social class. It's not a battle which can be won by defeating a privileged or a hostile enemy. All the people who live in an unjust system suffer from it, wherever they happen to fall in the hierarchy and whether they recognize their liability or not. They – we – are all in this together. The struggle for justice is a struggle to transform ourselves and the world around us into a mirror for those divine truths by which a just society is sustained.

One of the most striking examples of this principle can be found in Shoghi Effendi's prescription for healing racism, which Bahá'ís consider to be America's most challenging issue. According to Shoghi Effendi, neither black nor white people can wait for some change in the other or try to tell the other how to respond. Race unity can only be accomplished if every individual takes personal responsibility for the issue.

> Let the white make a supreme effort in their resolve to contribute their share to the solution of this problem, to abandon once for all their usually inherent and at times subconscious sense of superiority, to correct their tendency towards revealing a patronizing attitude towards the members of the other race, to persuade them through their intimate, spontaneous and informal association with them of the genuineness of their friendship and the sincerity of their intentions, and to master their impatience of any lack of responsiveness on the part of a people who have received, for so long a period, such grievous and slow-healing wounds. Let the Negroes, through a corresponding effort on their part, show by every means in their power the warmth of their response, their readiness to forget the past, and their ability to wipe out every trace of suspicion that may still linger in their hearts and minds. Let neither think that the solution of so vast a problem is a matter that exclusively concerns the other. Let neither think that such a problem can either easily or immediately be resolved. Let neither think that they can wait confidently for the solution of this problem until the initiative has been taken, and the favourable circumstances created, by agencies that stand outside the orbit of their Faith. Let neither think that anything short of genuine love, extreme patience, true humility, consummate tact, sound initiative, mature wisdom, and deliberate, persistent, and prayerful effort, can succeed in blotting out the stain which this patent evil has left on the fair name of their common country.[29]

Dr Ann Schoonmaker, in her essay 'Revisioning the Women's Movement', argues that the women's movement has adopted the vision of the patriarchal system it was created to change. Rather than merely fighting to win a place in a system that's failed, she suggests, people committed to women's rights should try to create a new system.

According to Dr Schoonmaker, women have traditionally seen four alternatives to patriarchy. They could 'stay in their place', accepting the inferior position that life seemed to have bequeathed for them. This is the lot of millions of poverty-stricken, illiterate women who are barely surviving while caught in a seemingly endless cycle of childbirth and child-death, often while still children themselves. They could conform to patriarchal assumptions by voluntarily playing a classical female role, in other words identifying with the aggressor. They could seek equal status within the patriarchal model to demand the males' prerogatives, which in a sense is another form of identifying with the aggressor. Or they could retreat to a vision of a past matriarchal age before the dominance of a masculine reality.

The problem with all of these options, Dr Schoonmaker explains, is that they all work within or against the patriarchal system. Why not work for a new system, in which no one is dominated or becomes dominant, in which every person, whether male or female, has an equal voice that does not require force to uphold it? This, she says, is the Bahá'í vision, 'the most radical revolution of all':

> It does not propose a cosmetic reform, but provides for a radical revisioning of our social structures. It does not call for remodelling society with patchwork or makeshift changes, nor does it tear down the world without knowing what shape and form the new structure will take. It is both a revisioning and a recreating of the very foundations of our being and becoming.[30]

Human Rights

Human rights are universal. They don't apply more or less to people from one culture or another. That was the point being made by Maryam Namazie, a Central Council Member of the London-based Organization of Women's Liberation and the Director of the

International Relations Committee of the Worker-Communist Party of Iran, when she wrote in October 2004 about 'the racist notion' that violence and misogyny in Iran 'is "our religion and culture"'.[31]

Still, there are many people who feel that abuses to people in other cultures can be justified based on the fact that those people are, well, from other cultures. For instance, it is sometimes suggested that clitorectomies (female genital mutilation) should not be considered abusive because it only seems wrong from the perspective of western culture: not only is it an accepted practice in other cultures, but it's perpetuated by women who themselves had clitorectomies when they were girls.

It should go without saying, although it apparently doesn't, that just because an activity is widely practised doesn't make it right. Every culture has contributions to make to the betterment of the world but no culture is perfect. As for why victims of abuse would become abusers themselves, it is unfortunately common for people to learn from and accept the practices that they grew up observing, and even for oppressed people to relish the assertion of minor acquisitions of power. It is also no secret that even in the United States abused children can be predisposed to grow up as abusive adults – but, because it happens in America, other Americans aren't as likely in those cases to say that it must be an acceptable cultural practice owing to the fact that the adults perpetrating the abuse already know what it's like to be abused and must have therefore found their abuse agreeable.

The fact that some people don't like being abused – for example, receiving clitorectomies – even if they come from cultures other than ours is demonstrated by the fact that there are people who try to flee these practices. Although not everyone who might want to escape from dangerous situations necessarily can, in 2002 the United Nations High Commissioner for Refugees was responsible for 20.6 million people 'of concern' who had run from or otherwise been displaced by conflicts, disasters and other devastating events.[32]

Cultures are different but the human need for security and

self-determination is universal. People, in other words, are people, even if they wear unfamiliar headgear.

One of the important advances in human rights discourse was the recognition of the rights of minority groups. This concept is expressed, for example, in the UN Declaration on the Rights of Persons Belonging to National or Ethnic, Religious or Linguistic Minorities (18 December 1992): 'States shall take measures to create favourable conditions to enable persons belonging to minorities to express their characteristics and to develop their culture, language, religion, traditions and customs . . .' These rights are essential for communities to self-organize and retain unique identities.

Unfortunately, in practice, the idea of 'minority rights' has become associated with a dangerous tendency for rights and privileges to be treated as commodities that can be alternatively extended or denied to certain groups, rather than as belonging intrinsically to each person. This is a tendency that has made its way into numerous state constitutions. Almost by default in the countries that are governed by such assumptions, an individual is not perceived as having any innate value beyond the ethnic or ideological categories to which he subscribes. This leaves no room for individuality or freedom of conscience, because he cannot define himself according to his own terms: to be legally sanctioned, he can only subscribe to a self-image that has already been promulgated by somebody else. This also creates the additional problem that groups are automatically aligned in adversarial relationships because their freedoms and prerogatives are defined by their relative strength. In addition, any group that does not meet the subjective standards of the decision-makers can be excluded from certain civil rights or any official recognition at all – a phenomenon that the Bahá'ís in Iran are well aware of.

'Abdu'l-Bahá states that all people share the same rights.

Equality and Brotherhood must be established among all members of mankind. This is according to Justice. The general rights of mankind must be guarded and preserved.

All men must be treated equally. This is inherent in the very nature of humanity.[33]

Bahá'u'lláh declares that our rights are granted by God, who knows no distinction between types of people.

> We remember every one of you, men and women, and from this Spot – the Scene of incomparable glory – regard you all as one soul and send you the joyous tidings of divine blessings which have preceded all created things, and of My remembrance that pervadeth everyone, whether young or old. The glory of God rest upon you, O people of Bahá. Rejoice with exceeding gladness through My remembrance, for He is indeed with you at all times.[34]

Many social change initiatives, when they reach a certain level of complexity, will find themselves confronted with questions of how people should govern themselves and how to engage with government structures that already exist. And these questions ultimately come down to our various understandings of human rights.

In the West, concepts of government are based on the idea that human rights are fundamental. John Locke, in his 'Second Treatise on Government', states that human beings made their start in a 'state of nature'. This is 'a *state of perfect freedom* to order their actions, and dispose of their possessions and persons, as they think fit, within the bounds of the law of nature, without asking leave, or depending upon the will of any other man . . .'[35]

> But though this be a *state of liberty*, yet it is not a *state of licence*: though man in that state has an uncontroulable liberty to dispose of his person or possessions, yet he has not the liberty to destroy himself, or so much as any creature in his possession, but where some nobler use than its bare preservation calls for it. The *state of nature* has a law of nature to govern it, which obliges every one: and reason, which is that law, teaches all mankind, who will but consult it, that being all *equal and independent*, no one ought to

harm another in his life, health, liberty, or possessions: for men being all the workmanship of one omnipotent, and infinitely wise maker; all the servants of one sovereign master, sent into the world by his order, and about his business; they are his property, whose workmanship they are, made to last during his, not one another's pleasure: and being furnished with like faculties, sharing all in one community of nature, there cannot be supposed any such *subordination* among us, that may authorize us to destroy one another, as if we were made for one another's uses, as the inferior ranks of creatures are for our's.[36]

This argument is at the foundation of contemporary political thought. Not all of the philosophers who inspired the Declaration of Independence, the US Constitution and its Bill of Rights always agreed with Locke, of course, but through all of their writings ran certain assumptions, or at least certain questions, which the founders of the United States took it upon themselves to address. And many of the concepts implicit in the Conventions and Declarations of the United Nations in support of international norms have emerged from the same philosophies, even when the United States itself has not ratified them.

Bahá'u'lláh declares that governments exist in part to safeguard the rights of humanity and that if they fail in this duty, they are answerable to God. 'God hath committed into your hands the reins of the government of the people, that ye may rule with justice over them, safeguard the rights of the down-trodden, and punish the wrong-doers. If ye neglect the duty prescribed unto you by God in His Book, your names shall be numbered with those of the unjust in His sight.'[37]

The aim of a Bahá'í activist is a just society. This can only be accomplished through a shift in paradigm. And, as the preceding passage from Locke indicates, the paradigm that informs our contemporary views of social order is based on what it means to be a human being – specifically, on the rights human beings have and the relationship between governments and the governed.

Some thinkers would say that human rights have evolved not

because of religion, but in spite of it. In his essay 'The Human Rights of Migrants: A Pastoral Challenge', Graziano Battistella summarizes the humanist argument that rejects a link between religion and rights (a position that is not his own): 'For instance, human rights support absolute freedom of conscience, while religions reject atheism; human rights require nondiscrimination, while religions admit distinctions based on religious adherence; human rights do not admit gender distinctions, while religions still maintain them.' In other words, 'religion is an alternative, and even competing ideology, to that of human rights.'[38]

Granting that there are differences of opinion, the discussion of spiritual reality is still inextricably linked to political discussions of human rights. Here is a crude explanation of this link in the West: God created human beings with certain rights over their own persons, well-being and property. Because every human is created by God, and every human is created by God with the same rights, no human may infringe on the personal integrity, well-being or property of another.

The fact that all people have rights implies that all rights are limited. Someone's right to the acquisition of property, for example, does not extend to the right to acquire someone else's property, because that person's rights are equal to his own. Therefore, the scope of all rights is circumscribed. There is no absolute freedom of action. Liberty is dependent on restraint, so that no one else's liberties are disrupted. Some thinkers have extended this idea to the conclusion that rights are intrinsically linked to responsibilities. In 1948, this concept was incorporated in the 'American Declaration on the Rights and Duties of Man'.

Because rights are the gift of God, they cannot justifiably be taken away by another power. However, in complex societies it is not possible for human beings to defend all of their rights on their own. Therefore, they establish governments to express their collective will by protecting the rights of all.

The reason a government has rights is that the people have lent it their rights. Thus, the rights belong fundamentally to the people, not the government. Should the government try to usurp rights which it has not been freely granted, it has overstepped its bounds and the citizens are justified in taking their conferred authority back from the government and selecting a new one in its stead.

Governments are not to be trusted. That is the concept behind the checks and balances of the federal government of the United States. James Madison wrote in 'The Federalist Papers' that 'the defect must be supplied, by so contriving the interior structure of the government as that its constituent parts may, by their mutual relations, be the means of keeping each other in their proper places'.[39]

When national governments come together to agree on international standards of behaviour, what they are implying is that human beings have inalienable rights which supersede the authority of states. Thus we have the Convention against Torture and Other Cruel, Inhuman or Degrading Treatment or Punishment; the Convention against Discrimination in Education; the Right to Organize and Collective Bargaining Convention; the Convention on the Political Rights of Women; the Declaration on the Elimination of All Forms of Racial Discrimination; the Convention on the Rights of the Child; and so on. The UN has consistently been used to declare that people must be treated with dignity wherever they live and whatever their local governments are like.

As we have seen, human rights are commonly thought of in terms of preventing people from violating each others' bodies, property and freedoms. The Bahá'í concept of human rights is broader: the spiritual nature of humanity, and humanity's intrinsic oneness, suggest that every person has a right to dignity and to realize his or her innate potential.[40]

When people are freed from the man-made dogmas that shackle them, they gain the freedom to develop their own latent capacities; and when previously disenfranchised groups begin taking their places alongside the rest of humanity, the impact will be unprecedented.

For example, according to the Bahá'í writings, the phenomenon of women exercising their rights on a vast scale is leading the world to peace. Partly, this is because peace is not possible in a world where injustice is perpetrated against half of the population. Partly, it is because every person and every group of people have things to contribute and some of the qualities which women can contribute are conducive to the elimination of armed conflict. In the words of 'Abdu'l-Bahá:

> When all mankind shall receive the same opportunity of education and the equality of men and women be realized, the foundations of war will be utterly destroyed. Without equality this will be impossible because all differences and distinction are conducive to discord and strife. Equality between men and women is conducive to the abolition of warfare for the reason that women will never be willing to sanction it.[41]

What diversity provides us with – the diversity of individuals, genders and cultures – is a multiplicity of experiences and viewpoints that broadens our collective perspective, provides us with more information with which to make decisions and has the potential to inspire unique contributions to our ever-advancing civilization.

As Dr Moojan Momen has pointed out, every time a new culture comes into contact with the Bahá'í Faith, it emphasizes those principles which are most relevant to its immediate needs. For many westerners that might be the principle of the harmony of science and religion. In eastern cultures it might be the importance of the family.[42] The interaction of different cultures helps a fuller picture of the religion to emerge. If certain cultures, or certain populations of certain cultures, are excluded from the dialogue, we are all impoverished.

'True liberty consisteth in man's submission unto My commandments, little as ye know it,' Bahá'u'lláh states in the Kitáb-i-Aqdas.[43]

The Bahá'í concept of liberty is not just about freedom but the acceptance by each individual of a divinely appointed sovereignty. It is about training the spiritual capacities that allow a person to play a positive role in her own and the world's advancement. It is freedom not from responsibility but from self-imposed limitation.

The Universal House of Justice explains that individual rights and responsibilities are at the heart of human development:

> How noteworthy that in the Order of Bahá'u'lláh, while the individual will is subordinated to that of society, the individual is not lost in the mass but becomes the focus of primary development, so that he may find his own place in the flow of progress, and society as a whole may benefit from the accumulated talents and abilities of the individuals composing it. Such an individual finds fulfilment of his potential not merely in satisfying his own wants but in realizing his completeness in being at one with humanity and with the divinely ordained purpose of creation.[44]

Women, Human Rights and Peace

The Bahá'í writings say that as women exercise their rights as full partners on the world stage, they bring the world close to peace. One interesting example of this trend was an anti-nuclear protest at Greenham Common in Berkshire, England, where women campaigned against the government's decision to deploy 96 US cruise missiles at the site. 'Men were discouraged from joining the women, who feared they would lend an aggressive edge to the peaceful protest,' read a *USA Today* report of the event. 'The Greenham women claimed success in 1992 when the last cruise missiles were moved out.'[45] And yet 'Abdu'l-Bahá did not claim that all women are pacifists. In New York in 1912, after explaining in a talk at a women's suffrage meeting that 'woman will be the obstacle and hindrance' to war, He told a story about a queen who heroically led her army in a fight against Roman legions.[46] Thus it's clear that He was not talking about a lack of ability but the addition of a new outlook.

Bibliography

'Abdu'l-Bahá. *Foundations of World Unity*. Wilmette, IL: Bahá'í Publishing Trust, 1945.
— *The Promulgation of Universal Peace*. Wilmette, IL: Bahá'í Publishing Trust, 1982.
— *The Secret of Divine Civilization*. Wilmette, IL: Bahá'í Publishing Trust, 1990.
'Abdu'l-Bahá in London. London: Bahá'í Publishing Trust, 1987.
Agence France Presse. 'India's untouchables forced out of relief camps'. 7 January 2005: http://story.news.yahoo.com/news?tmpl=story&ci d=1535&e=3&u=/afp/20050107/wl_sthasia_afp/asiaquakeindiauntouchables
— 'Scientists get to work on early warning system after tsunami disaster'. 18 January 2005: http://story.news.yahoo.com/news?tmpl=story&cid =1503&ncid=1503&e=2&u=/afp/20050118/ts_afp/asiaquakeundisaster_050118171639
Ahmadiyeh, Dr Hidayatu'lláh. Talk at Bahá'í Youth Conference. Juarez, Mexico, July 1988.
The Albuquerque Journal. Saturday, 28 November 1988, p. A2.
Allmart, William. Personal interviews, 2004.
Anello, Dr Eloy and Joan Barstow Hernández. *Moral Leadership*. Santa Cruz, Bolivia: Núr University.
Arbab, Dr Farzam. 'Promoting a Discourse on Science, Religion, and Development'. Sharon M.P. Harper (ed.). *The Lab, the Temple and the Market*. Ottawa: International Development Research Centre, 2000.
Association for the Cohesive Development of the Amazon. *Programme Summary*. 2002.
Bahá'í International Community. 'Bahá'í Development Projects: A Global Process of Learning'. 2002: http://www.bahai.org/article-1-8-1-1.html

— '. . . for the betterment of the world'. New York: Bahá'í International Community, 2002.

— Sustainable Communities in an Integrating World. New York: Bahá'í International Community, 1996.

— Turning Point for All Nations: A Statement of the Bahá'í International Community on the Occasion of the 50th Anniversary of the United Nations. New York: Bahá'í International Community United Nations Office, 1995.

— Valuing Spirituality in Development. London: Bahá'í Publishing Trust, 1998.

'Bahá'í Social and Economic Development: Prospects for the Future'. A statement approved by the Universal House of Justice for use in orienting and guiding the work of Bahá'í social and economic development throughout the world, 16 September 1993 (also in Readings on Bahá'í Social and Economic Development, pp. 11, 15).

The Bahá'í World. vol. 17. Haifa: Bahá'í World Centre, 1981.

Bahá'í World Faith. Wilmette, IL: Bahá'í Publishing Trust, 2nd edn. 1976.

Bahá'u'lláh. Epistle to the Son of the Wolf. Wilmette, IL: Bahá'í Publishing Trust, 1988.

— Gleanings from the Writings of Bahá'u'lláh. Wilmette, IL: Bahá'í Publishing Trust, 1983.

— The Hidden Words. Wilmette, IL: Bahá'í Publishing Trust, 1990.

— The Kitáb-i-Aqdas. Haifa: Bahá'í World Centre, 1992.

— Kitáb-i-Íqán. Wilmette, IL: Bahá'í Publishing Trust, 1989.

— The Proclamation of Bahá'u'lláh. Haifa: Bahá'í World Centre, 1967.

— The Summons of the Lord of Hosts: Tablets of Bahá'u'lláh. Haifa: Bahá'í World Centre, 2002.

— Tablets of Bahá'u'lláh. Wilmette, IL: Bahá'í Publishing Trust, 1988.

The Bangkok Post. http://search.bangkokpost.co.th/bkkpost/2000/bp2000_jun/bp20000602/020600_business01.html

Battistella, Graziano, c.s. 'The Human Rights of Migrants: A Pastoral Challenge'. Migration, Religious Experience, and Globalization. New York: Center for Migration Studies, 2003, p. 92.

'"Beach angel" praised for her quick actions'. IOL, 1 January 2005: http://www.iol.co.za/index.php?set_id=1&click_id=126&art_id=qw1104573780469B221

Beckett, Sister Wendy. Sister Wendy's Story of Painting. New York: DK Publishing, 1994.

Billimoria, Roshan R., for the National Board, YWCA of the U.S.A. *Translating Global Concern into Local Community Programs: Women's Mid-Decade Dialogue.* New York: National Board, YWCA, 1983.

Borlaug, Norman. 'Biotechnology and the Green Revolution'. ActionBioscence.org. http://www.actionbioscience.org/biotech/borlaug.html

Bowden, Mark. 'Among the Hostage-Takers'. *The Atlantic Monthly,* December 2004, p. 78.

Brockerhoff, Martin P. 'An Urbanizing World'. *Population Bulletin,* vol. 55, no. 3, September 2000: http://www.prb.org/Template.cfm?Sectio n=PRB&template=/ContentManagement/ContentDisplay.cfm&Cont entID=2997#urbanpoptrends

Buckley, Steven. 'The Littlest Laborers: Why Does Child Labor Continue to Thrive in the Developing World?' *The Washington Post.* 16 March 2000. Reprinted on the Global Policy Forum website, http://www.globalpolicy.org/globaliz/econ/kidlabor.htm

Bury, J.B. *The Invasion of Europe by the Barbarians.* New York: W. W. Norton & Company, 2000.

Calvary Prophecy website: http://www.calvaryprophecy.com/

Carlson, Emily. 'Study shows that genes can protect kids against poverty'. The University of Wisconsin-Madison: University Communications, 25 May 2004: http://www.news.wisc.edu/9853.html

Central Intelligence Agency. *The World Factbook.* 2004: http://www.cia. gov/cia/publications/factbook/

The Compilation of Compilations. Prepared by the Universal House of Justice 1963-1990. 2 vols. [Mona Vale NSW]: Bahá'í Publications Australia, 1991.

Conservation of the Earth's Resources. Compilation of the Research Department of the Universal House of Justice. London: Bahá'í Publishing Trust, 1990.

Coulon, Jocelyn. *The Globe and Mail.* Reprinted in *World Press Review,* May 2000, p. 20.

Dahl, Arthur Lyon. *The Eco Principle: Ecology and Economics in Symbiosis.* Oxford: George Ronald; London: Zed Books, 1996.

— 'Sustainable Development and the Environment of the World: An Overview'. Talk delivered at the International Bahá'í Environment Conference, de Poort, Netherlands, 24-6 October 1997. http://bahai-library.org/conferences/sustainable.development.html

Davis, William E. and Shahla Maghzi. 'Learning about the Application of Principle-Based Indicators of Development: Evaluating Community-based Natural Resource Decision Making in Latin America'. Presentation at the Association for Bahá'í Studies–North America 27th Annual Conference: Religion and Community in a Time of Crisis. 29 August – 1 September 2003, Burlingame, California.

'Destitution not Dearth'. *The Economist*, 20 August 2005, p. 57.

Diamond, Jared. *Collapse: How Societies Choose to Fail or Succeed*. New York: Viking, 2005.

— *Guns, Germs, and Steel*. New York: W. W. Norton & Company, 1997.

Diouf, Nafi. 'Niger Struggles to Find Hunger Solutions'. Associated Press, 12 August 2005: http://news.yahoo.com/s/ap/20050812/ap_on_re_af/niger_hunger_1;_ylt=Ak66T_iCtaY7QTYApkfsvUPeAZkv;_ylu=X3oDMTBiMW04NW9mBHNlYwMlJVRPUCUl (last accessed 12 August 2005).

'Doing well and doing good'. *The Economist*, 31 July – 6 August 2004.

Dorsey, David. 'Positive Deviant'. *Fast Company*, issue 41, December 2000, p. 284. http://pf.fastcompany.com/magazine/41/sternin.html

Eaves, Elisabeth. 'Dispatches From Yemen: The Judge Who Converts Terrorists'. *Slate*, 18 May 2004: http://slate.msn.com/id/2100581/entry/2100586/

Ellison, R. Weslie. 'Logic Model Matrix'. December 2004.

'Empty bowls, heads and pockets'. *The Economist*, 31 July – 6 August 2004.

Encyclopaedia Britannica, 11th ed. http://www.1911encyclopedia.org (see 'Ferrera-Florence, Council of').

Evans, R. J. W. and Hartmut Pogge von Strandmann (eds.). *The Coming of the First World War*. Oxford: Clarendon Press, 1990. (Paperback with corrections; 1991 reprinting.)

'Facts on children'. UNICEF website: http://www.unicef.org/media/media_fastfacts.html (last accessed 29 July 2005).

'Food for Thought'. *The Economist*, 31 July – 6 August 2004.

'Food For Thought for Your Communications Planning'. *Profiles in Communications*, vol. 2, no. 7, July 2003.

Foundations for a Spiritual Education: Research of the Bahá'í Writings, prepared by the National Bahá'í National Education Task Force of the National Spiritual Assembly of the Bahá'ís of the United States. Wilmette, IL: Bahá'í Publishing Trust.

Friedman, Thomas L. *The Lexus and the Olive Tree*. New York: Anchor Books, 2000.

Fukuyama, Francis. 'Nation-Building 101'. *The Atlantic Monthly*, January/February 2004, pp. 159–62.

Gamel, Kim. 'U.N. Adopts Economic Resolution on Sudan'. Associated Press, 30 July 2004. http://story.news.yahoo.com/news?tmpl=story&cid=535&ncid=535&e=6&u=/ap/20040730/ap_on_re_mi_ea/un_sudan_39

Gandhi, Mohandas. From *The Diary of Mahadev Desai*.

— From *Young India*, 17 July 1924.

Gannon, Kathy. 'Interest in Kabul orphanage wanes, but needy kids remain'. Associated Press, 16 November 2002.

Grayzel, Solomon. *A History of the Jews*. New York: Mentor, 1968.

'Green Revolution'. Wikipedia. http://en.wikipedia.org/wiki/Green_revolution

Gribbin, John. *Schrödinger's Kittens and the Search for Reality*. New York: Little, Brown and Company, 1995.

Hanson, Holly. 'Clay into Crystal: How Thought Shapes Structure in the Pursuit of Justice'. Talk delivered to the Association for Bahá'í Studies, Seattle, 1 September 2001. http://bahai-library.org/conferences/clay.crystal.html

— 'Global Dilemmas, Local Responses: Creating Patterns of Action that Make the World Different'. Talk delivered at the Bahá'í Development Conference for the Americas, Orlando, Florida, December 2000: http://bahai-library.org/conferences/global.dilemmas.html (last accessed 16 July 2005).

Hanson Vick, Holly. *Social and Economic Development: A Bahá'í Approach*. Oxford: George Ronald, 1989.

Hartung, Jessica. *Non-Profit Management: Creating Change, Starting Within*. Boulder, CO: Integrated Work Strategies, LLC.

Health for Humanity 2002 Annual Report: http://www.healthforhumanity.org/

Health for Humanity Policy Procedures: http://www.healthforhumanity.org/

'Health for Humanity: It takes a global village . . . to unite around a global vision', 2002: http://www.healthforhumanity.org/

The Heart of the Lotus. Toronto: Asterisk Films. 1987.

Hirsh, Michael. 'What are We Fighting For?' *Newsweek*, 24 April 2000.

Hitler, Adolf. *Mein Kampf.*

Hollender, Jeffrey. Talk at Northwestern University, Evanston, IL, 10 March 2004.

Holy Bible, King James Version.

Hussein, Adil. 'Dimensions of independent socio-economic development'. Mazin Al-Najjar, PhD (ed.). Muslimedia International, July 2004: http://www.muslimedia.com/socioecon-adil.htm

'In India, a program for rural women emphasizes training as the key to effective use of solar cookers'. *One Country*, October – December 2002: http://www.onecountry.org/e143/e14304as_Barli_Solar_story. htm

Inter-Agency Secretariat of the International Strategy for Disaster Reduction (UN/ISDR). 'Global Early Warning System Launched at Conference on Disaster Reduction', 19 January 2005.

International Institute for Sustainable Development. 'Full Text of the Bellagio Principles'. http://www.iisd.org/measure/principles/bp_full. asp

ISED Solutions. 'Diversifying Agency Funding'. *Refugee Assets*, vol. 3, issue 1, March 2004.

Javid, Mahnaz A. Personal interview, 19 March 2004.

Jensen, Mehri Samandari, EdD. 'Religion and Family Planning in Contemporary Iran'. Peter Smith, PhD (ed.). *In Iran*. Los Angeles: Kalimát Press, 1986.

Johnson, Rev. George, PhD, Rev. Jerome D. Hannon, PhD, JCD. and Sister M. Dominica, OSU, PhD. *The Story of the Church*. New York: Benziger Brothers, 1935.

Kahane, Howard. *Logic and Contemporary Rhetoric*. Belmont, CA: Wadsworth Publishing, 1992.

Kaplan, Robert D. 'Five Days in Fallujah'. *The Atlantic Monthly*, July/ August 2004, p. 120.

Keats, Jonathon. 'Copy This Article and Win Quick Cash!' *Wired*, issue 12.07, July 2004.

Khadem, May, MD, MPH. 'Blindness Prevention Projects'. Talk at Health for Humanity Conference, National-Louis University, Evanston, Illinois, 19 June 2004.

Khan, Peter J. Talk at the Baháʼí Centre in Sydney, Australia, 30 November 2003.

Kingdon, Geeta Gandhi. 'Women, Education and Development'. Seena

Fazel and John Danesh (eds.). *Reason and Revelation*. Los Angeles: Kalimát Press, 2002, pp. 231–43.

Klein, Naomi. 'Baghdad Year Zero'. *Harper's Magazine*, September 2004.

LaFever, Marcella. *Increasing Hmong Co-Culture Participation in Community Decision Making: A Case Study for Third-Culture Building in the Sacramento Bahá'í Community*. Dissertation. California State University, 2002.

LaFraniere, Sharon. 'Cellphones Catapult Rural Africa to 21st Century'. *New York Times*, 25 August 2005: http://www.nytimes. com/2005/08/25/international/africa/25africa.html (last accessed 26 August 2005).

Lairson, Thomas D. and David Skidmore. *International Political Economy: The Struggle for Power and Wealth*. New York: Harcourt Brace College Publishers, 1993, pp. 259–61.

Langewiesche, William. 'The Accuser'. *The Atlantic Monthly*, March 2005, p. 72.

Lawson, Christiana. Personal interview, 24 March 2004.

'Lifting Trade Barriers Would Reduce Poverty – Study'. Reuters, 17 June 2004: http://story.news.yahoo.com/news?tmpl=story&cid=574&e=1 6&u=/nm/20040618/wl_nm/trade_doha_study_dc

Lights of Guidance: A Bahá'í Reference File. Compiled by Helen Hornby. New Delhi: Bahá'í Publishing Trust, 5th edn. 1997.

Locke, John. 'Second Treatise on Government'. http://libertyonline. hypermall.com/Locke/second/second-frame.html (last accessed 14 August 2005).

'Love and Genes Can Beat Poverty – Study'. Reuters, 26 May 2004: http://story.news.yahoo.com/news?tmpl=story&cid=570&e=10&u=/ nm/20040526/sc_nm/science_poverty_dc_1

Manning, Richard. 'The Oil We Eat'. *Harper's*, February 2004.

McKenzie, Glenn. 'Faith, politics threaten effort against polio'. *Chicago Tribune*. 12 February 2004, section 1, p. 29.

Mehra, Preeti. 'Leading from the Bottom'. *World Press Review*, June 2000, p. 14.

Menking, Cornell Howard. 'Programa Liderazgo Educativo, Ecuador: A Qualitative Case Study of an Experiment in Transformational Leadership, Education and Community Development'.

Miller-Muro, Layli. Personal interview, 5 December 2003.

Mohajer, Nicole. Personal interviews, 1994.

Mohajer, Sohayl. Personal interviews, 1994.

Mohan, Vasu. Personal interview, 6 March 2004.

Momen, Moojan. 'A Change of Culture'. Published on the Internet in February 2003 and updated in September 2004.

— 'Learning from History'. *Journal of Bahá'í Studies*, vol. 2, no. 2 (1989–90).

— 'Reformulating the Bahá'í Faith: An approach to teaching Chinese peoples'. Talk at the European Symposium on Teaching the Chinese held at De Poort, Netherlands, 8–11 September 1988; the talk was published in *European Symposium on Teaching the Chinese* shortly thereafter.

The Mona Foundation website: http://www.monafoundation.org

Mroue, Bassem. 'Gunmen Kill Three Iraqi Candidates'. Associated Press, 18 January 2005: http://story.news.yahoo.com/news?tmpl=story&cid =514&e=2&u=/ap/20050118/ap_on_re_mi_ea/iraq_050118185118

Muḥammad. Prophet Muḥammad's Charter of Privileges, written 628 AD. See English translation by Dr A. Zahoor and Dr Z. Haq at http://www.cyberistan.org/islamic/charter1.html (last accessed 14 August 2005).

Mundy, Alicia. 'Risk Management'. *Harper's Magazine*, Sept. 2004.

Nabíl-i-Aʻẓam. *The Dawn-Breakers: Nabíl's Narrative of the Early Days of the Bahá'í Revelation*. Wilmette, IL: Bahá'í Publishing Trust, 1970.

Namazie, Maryam. 'Saying no'. iranian.com. 12 October 2004.

National Society of Fundraising Professionals. 'Position Paper: Percentage-Based Compensation'. 1992: http://www.nsfre.org/tier3_cd.cfm?folder_id=899&content_item_id=1227

National Spiritual Assembly of the Bahá'ís of the United States. *Five Year Plan: 2001–2006 – Junior Youth*. Wilmette, IL: National Spiritual Assembly of the Bahá'ís of the United States, 2001.

— *Unity and Consultation: Foundations of Sustainable Community Development*.

New Straits Times. Kuala Lumpur, 14 April 2000, quoted in *World Press Review*, June 2000, p. 4.

Noguchi, Lori. Personal interview, 29 October 2003.

Oguz, Ömer. 'Niger: 2004 World Press Freedom Review'. International Press Institute website: http://www.freemedia.at/wpfr/Africa/niger.htm (last accessed 9 September 2005).

O'Reilly, Finbarr. 'Congo death toll: 2,500 per day'. *Toronto Star*, 25 May 2003.

Pink, Daniel H. 'The New Face of the Silicon Age'. *Wired*, February 2004.

Public Citizen. 'FDA Should Immediately Ban Dangerous Diet Drug Meridia', 19 March 2002: http://www.citizen.org/pressroom/release.cfm?ID=1059

Publius (James Madison, Alexander Hamilton and John Jay). Mitchell Cohen and Nicole Fermon (eds.). 'The Federalist Papers'. *Princeton Readings in Political Thought*. New Jersey: Princeton University Press, 1996. See also http://www.foundingfathers.info/federalistpapers/fed-index.htm (last accessed 14 August 2005).

Raghavan, Sudarsan. 'UN officials stunned to find refugee camp emptied in Sudan'. *Chicago Tribune*, 2 July 2004: http://story.news.yahoo.com/news?tmpl=story&cid=2027&ncid=2027&e=6&u=/chitribts/20040702/ts_chicagotrib/unofficialsstunnedtofindrefugee-campemptiedinsudan

Readings on Bahá'í Social and Economic Development. Riviera Beach, FL: Palabra Publications, 2000.

'Reproduction and Other Biological Subjects'. (Extracts from letters written on behalf of Shoghi Effendi and the Universal House of Justice, unpublished). http://bahai-library.com/?file=uhj_reproduction.html

Reynolds, Samantha. 'Home-grown Government'. *Aina*, Winter 1996–7, vol. 1, no. 3.

Roberts, J. M. *The Penguin History of the World*. London: Penguin Books, 1995.

Rohde, David. 'In Sri Lanka's Time of Agony, a Moment of Peace'. *The New York Times*, 4 January 2005.

Sami, Mojgan. 'Measuring Development'. Workshop at the Bahá'í Conference on Social and Economic Development, Orlando, Florida, December 2004.

— Personal interviews, 30 March and 2 April 2004.

Save the Children. *State of the World's Mothers*. Connecticut: Save the Children, 2003.

Schaffter, Tim. 'Activities Report: Refugee Camps, Thailand'. 20 April 1986.

Schoonmaker, Ann, PhD. 'Revisioning the Women's Movement'. Anthony Lee (ed.). *Circle of Unity*. Kalimát Press, 1984.

Schuller, Sabine. Personal interview, 22 December 2003.

Secor, Laura. 'The Pragmatist'. *The Atlantic Monthly*, July/August 2004.

Shoghi Effendi. *The Advent of Divine Justice*. Wilmette, IL: Bahá'í Publishing Trust, 1990.

— *High Endeavors: Messages to Alaska*. [Anchorage]: National Spiritual

Assembly of the Baháʼís of Alaska, 1976.

— *The World Order of Baháʼuʼlláh*. Wilmette, IL: Baháʼí Publishing Trust, 1991.

Smee, Jesse. 'Women end 19-year anti-nuclear protest'. *USA Today*, 6 September 2000, p. 13A.

Smith, Adam. *Wealth of Nations*. New York: Modern Library, 1937.

Srouji, Esther. Personal interview, 1993.

Stockman, Dr Robert. Personal interviews, 2004.

Surowiecki, James. *The Wisdom of Crowds*. New York: Doubleday, 2004.

Taherzadeh, Adib. *The Revelation of Baháʼuʼlláh*, vol. 4, ch. 22. Oxford: George Ronald, 1987.

Transparency International. *Global Corruption Report 2003*: http://www.globalcorruptionreport.org/gcr2003.htm

Tréan, Claire. *Le Monde*, 24 May 2000. Reprinted in *World Press Review*, August 2000, p. 16.

Treaty Between the United States of America and the Navajo Tribe of Indians/With a Record of the Discussions that Led to its Signing. Las Vegas: KC Publications, 1968.

UNHCR. '2003: The Year in Review'. *Refugees*, vol. 4, no. 133, 2003.

United Way website: http://www.unitedway.org/outcomes

The Universal House of Justice. *Century of Light*. Wilmette, IL: Baháʼí Publishing Trust, 2001.

— *The Constitution of the Universal House of Justice*. Haifa: Baháʼí World Centre, 1972.

— *Individual Rights and Freedoms in the World Order of Baháʼuʼlláh*. Wilmette, IL: Baháʼí Publishing Trust, 1989.

— Letter of 20 October 1983.

— Letter written on behalf of the Universal House of Justice to an individual, 5 June 1988: http://bahai-library.com/?file=uhj_legislating_morality.html

— Letter to an individual, 23 August 2001: http://bahai-library.com/uhj/stem.cells.html

— Letter to the Followers of Baháʼuʼlláh in the Cradle of the Faith, dated the Day of the Covenant, 26 November 2003.

— 'The Challenge and Promise of Baháʼí Scholarship'. *Baháʼí World*, vol. 17, pp. 195–6.

— *The Promise of World Peace*. London: Oneworld Publications, 1986.

Vakil, Anna C. 'Natural Stirrings at the Grassroots: Development,

Doctrine, and the Dignity Principle'. *The Journal of Bahá'í Studies*, vol. 11, no. 1, February 2001, pp. 23–76.

Van der Essen, L. 'The Council of Florence'. *The Catholic Encyclopedia* Vol. 6, 1914: http://www.newadvent.org/

Vanguard Communications. 'Food For Thought for Your Communications Planning'. *Profiles in Communications*, vol. 2, no. 7, July 2003.

— 'Measuring Outcomes'. *Profiles in Communications*, vol. 2, no. 7, July 2003.

Verderoon, Wally. 'Grant Writing 101'. Talk at Health for Humanity Conference, National-Louis University, Evanston, Illinois, 19 June 2004.

Waite, Anne. Personal interview, 1996.

Waite, Stephen. Personal interview, 1996.

Washington, Bill. Email, 18 March 2004.

Washington, George. Farewell Address, 17 September 1796.

Wax, Emily. 'In Sudan, Death and Denial: Officials Accused of Concealing Crisis as Thousands Starve'. *Chicago Tribune*, 27 June 2004, p. A1.

Weinberg, Matthew. Discussion, August 2004.

Welch, David. 'California Rules, Detroit Quakes'. *BusinessWeek*, 12 July 2004, pp. 36–7.

White, Robert A. *Spiritual Foundations for an Ecologically Sustainable Society*. Ottawa: Bahá'í Studies Publications, 1998.

World Bank. 'Draft and background papers of the World Bank's Policy Research Report on Gender and Development': http://www.worldbank.org/gender/prr

— World Development Indicators database, September 2004: http://www.worldbank.org/data/quickreference/quickref.html

World Center on Disaster Reduction Secretariat. *Program: World Conference on Disaster Reduction, 18–22 January 2005, Kobe, Hyogo, Japan*: http://www.unisdr.org/wcdr/

World Press Review. May 2000, June 2000, August 2000 and August 2001.

'The World This Week'. *The Economist*, 31 July – 6 August 2004.

Worldwatch Institute. *State of the World 2003*. New York: W. W. Norton & Company, 2003.

Yoon, Soo-Jin. Personal interview, 2004.

References and Notes

1. Bahá'u'lláh, *Tablets*, p. 167.
2. 'Abdu'l-Bahá, *Promulgation*, p. 8.
3. The Universal House of Justice, 'The Challenge and Promise of Bahá'í Scholarship', in *Bahá'í World*, vol. 17, p. 195.
4. The Universal House of Justice, *Individual Rights and Freedoms*, para. 51.
5. Peter Khan. Talk given at the Bahá'í Centre in Sydney, 30 November 2003.
6. Personal interview with Vasu Mohan, 6 March 2004.
7. Hanson Vick, *Social and Economic Development*, p. 10.
8. Personal interview with Mahnaz Javid, 19 March 2004.

Chapter 1

1. 'Doing well and doing good', *The Economist*, 31 July–6 August 2004, p. 58. According to *The Economist*, the study 'suggests', as opposed to conclusively proves, that religious people give more.
2. Jensen, 'Religion and Family Planning in Contemporary Iran', in *In Iran*, p. 228.
3. Bahá'u'lláh, *Tablets*, p. 96.
4. Taherzadeh, *Revelation of Bahá'u'lláh*, vol. 4, ch. 22.
5. Bahá'u'lláh, *Tablets*, pp. 92–3.
6. The Crimson Book is identified by Bahá'u'lláh as the Kitáb-i-'Ahdí, 'the Book of My Covenant', Bahá'u'lláh's will and testament. It can be found in *Tablets of Bahá'u'lláh Revealed after the Kitáb-i-Aqdas*, p. 217.
7. Bahá'u'lláh, *Tablets*, pp. 89–90.
8. Personal interview with Mahnaz A. Javid, 19 March 2004.
9. 'Empty bowls, heads and pockets', *The Economist*, 31 July – 6 August 2004, p. 21.
10. 'Food for Thought', ibid. p. 68.

11. Roberts, *Penguin History of the World*, pp. 678–83.
12. ibid. pp. 966–7.
13. Manning, 'The Oil We Eat', *Harper's*, February 2004, p. 42.
14. Brockerhoff, 'An Urbanizing World', *Population Bulletin*, vol. 55, no. 3, September 2000.
15. Bahá'u'lláh, *Tablets*, p. 144.
16. 'Green Revolution'. Wikipedia. http://en.wikipedia.org/wiki/Green_ revolution
17. Borlaug, 'Biotechnology and the Green Revolution'. ActionBioscence. org. http://www.actionbioscience.org/biotech/borlaug.html
18. For example, see Bahá'u'lláh, *Tablets*, p. 22, for a discussion on the intended impact of an international auxiliary language. This topic is also addressed later in the chapter.
19. 'Food for Thought', *The Economist*, 31 July – 6 August 2004, p. 69. 'Famine' is a specific term; in August 2005 the UN announced that the combined effects of drought and locusts had left about 3.6 million people in Niger facing severe food shortages, and the Associated Press observed that 40 per cent of children showed signs of malnutrition even at the best of times. However, wrote the Associated Press, 'U.N. experts . . . have been careful to say that while the situation is dire across the region, it has not yet reached famine proportions.' Nevertheless, the relationship of food distribution with media openness is easy to see, as this statement from the Associated Press reveals: '[The president of Niger] played down the food crisis in an interview with the BBC this week, saying his people "look well-fed" – even as TV networks broadcast images of severely malnourished, skeletal children in eastern Niger' (Diouf, 'Niger Struggles to Find Hunger Solutions'. Associated Press. 12 August 2005: http://news.yahoo.com/s/ap/20050812/ap_on_re_af/ niger_hunger_1;_ylt=Ak66T_iCtaY7QTYApkfsvUPeAZkv;_ylu=X3o DMTBiMW04NW9mBHNlYwMlJVRPUCUl (last accessed 12 August 2005).

According to the International Press Institute, progress toward press freedom in Niger has been slow (Oguz, 'Niger: 2004 World Press Freedom Review'. International Press Institute Website: http://www. freemedia.at/wpfr/Africa/niger.htm (last accessed 9 September 2005). Regardless of the cause, what's clear is that the troubles in Niger extend beyond a lack of food – the 2005 cereal harvest in Niger was actually 22 per cent greater than in 2000–1, a year that passed without a food crisis in the country. ('Destitution not Dearth', *The Economist*, 20 August 2005, p. 57).

20. Bahá'u'lláh, *Tablets*, p. 40.

21. 'Food for Thought', *The Economist*, 31 July – 6 August 2004, p. 69.

22. 'Abdu'l-Bahá, *Promulgation*, p. 122.

23. Cited in the Universal House of Justice, *Promise of World Peace with Quotations*, p. 77.

24. O'Reilly, 'Congo death toll: 2,500 per day', *Toronto Star*, 25 May 2003: http://www.thestar.com/NASApp/cs/ContentServer?pagename=thestar/Layout/Article_Type1&c=Article&cid=1052251651689&call_pageid=968332188854&col=968350060724 (last accessed 14 August 2005).

25. The Universal House of Justice, *Promise of World Peace*, para. 2.

26. Evans and Pogge von Strandmann, *Coming of the First World War*, p. 54.

27. Letter from the Universal House of Justice to the Followers of Bahá'u'lláh in the Cradle of the Faith, 26 November 2003.

28. Shoghi Effendi, *World Order*, p. 45.

29. 'Abdu'l-Bahá, *Promulgation*, p. 469.

30. ibid. pp. 181–2.

31. Adolf Hitler, quoted in the Universal House of Justice, *Promise of World Peace with Quotations*, p. 91.

32. Bahá'u'lláh, *Tablets*, p. 165.

33. ibid.

34. Coulon, *The Globe and Mail*. Reprinted in *World Press Review*, May 2000, p. 20.

35. 'Abdu'l-Bahá, *Promulgation*, p. 122.

36. Tréan, *Le Monde*, 24 May 2000. Reprinted in *World Press Review*, August 2000, p. 16.

37. Bahá'í International Community, *Turning Point for All Nations*, p. 11.

38. ibid. p. 8.

39. Personal interviews with Mojgan Sami, 30 March and 2 April 2004.

40. Reuters, 'Lifting Trade Barriers Would Reduce Poverty – Study.' 17 June 2004. http://story.news.yahoo.com/news?tmpl=story&cid=574&e=16&u=/nm/20040618/wl_nm/trade_doha_study_dc

41. Quoted in LaFever, *Hmong Co-Culture Participation*, pp. 85–6.

42. Bahá'u'lláh, *Tablets*, p. 90.

43. ibid. p. 127.

44. Bowden, 'Among the Hostage-Takers', *The Atlantic Monthly*,

December 2004, p. 78.

45. Reprinted in *World Press Review*, August 2001, p. 11.
46. Friedman, *Lexus and the Olive Tree*, pp. xvi–xvii.
47. Shoghi Effendi, *World Order*, p. 203.
48. ibid. p. 204.
49. Bahá'u'lláh, *Tablets*, p. 94.
50. 'Abdu'l-Baha, in *Bahá'í World Faith*, p. 411.
51. Bahá'u'lláh, *Hidden Words*, Arabic no. 2.
52. Kahane, *Logic and Contemporary Rhetoric*, p. 84.
53. Bahá'u'lláh, *Tablets*, p. 22.
54. Mundy, 'Risk Management', *Harper's Magazine*, September 2004, p. 83; Public Citizen, 'FDA Should Immediately Ban Dangerous Diet Drug Meridia', 19 March 2002: http://www.citizen.org/pressroom/release.cfm?ID=1059
55. Mroue, 'Gunmen Kill Three Iraqi Candidates', Associated Press, 18 January 2005: http://story.news.yahoo.com/news?tmpl=story&cid=514&e=2&u=/ap/20050118/ap_on_re_mi_ea/iraq_050118185118
56. Publius, 'The Federalist Papers', *Princeton Readings in Political Thought*, pp. 338–40.
57. McKenzie, 'Faith, politics threaten effort against polio', *Chicago Tribune*, 12 February 2004, section 1, p. 29.
58. Personal interview with Vasu Mohan, 6 March 2004.
59. 'India's untouchables forced out of relief camps', Agence France Presse, 7 January 2005. http://story.news.yahoo.com/news?tmpl=story&cid=1535&e=3&u=/afp/20050107/wl_sthasia_afp/asiaquakeindiauntouchables
60. Rohde, 'In Sri Lanka's Time of Agony, a Moment of Peace', *The New York Times*, 4 January 2005.
61. World Conference on Disaster Reduction Secretariat. World Conference on Disaster Reduction programme, 18–22 January 2005, Kobe, Hyogo, Japan. http://www.unisdr.org/wcdr/
62. 'Scientists get to work on early warning system after tsunami disaster', Agence France Presse, 18 January 2005. http://story.news.yahoo.com/news?tmpl=story&cid=1503&ncid=1503&e=2&u=/afp/20050118/ts_afp/asiaquakeundisaster_050118171639
63. Inter-Agency Secretariat of the International Strategy for Disaster Reduction (UN/ISDR), 'Global Early Warning System Launched at Conference on Disaster Reduction', 19 January 2005.

64. Personal interview with Vasu Mohan, 6 March 2004.
65. Bahá'u'lláh, *Gleanings*, p. 260.
66. 'Facts on children', UNICEF website: http://www.unicef.org/media/media_fastfacts.html (last accessed 29 July 2005).
67. The Mona Foundation website: http://www.monafoundation.org/
68. Personal interview with Sohayl Mohajer, 1994.
69. 'Abdu'l-Baha, *Secret of Divine Civilization*, p. 18.
70. 'Abdu'l-Bahá, *Promulgation*, p. 318.
71. ibid. p. 175.
72. Save the Children, *State of the World's Mothers*, pp. 33, 38.
73. Kingdon, 'Women, Education and Development', in Fazel and Sanesh, *Reason and Revelation*, p. 238.
74. '"Beach angel" praised for her quick actions', IOL, 1 January 2005: http://www.iol.co.za/index.php?set_id=1&click_id=126&art_id=qw1104573780469B221
75. Paraphrased from the words of 'Abdu'l-Bahá, in *Star of the West*, vol. 9, no. 3, p. 30.
76. Personal interview with Stephen Waite, 1996. The field of Bahá'í education is vast and constantly growing. Anyone looking for an introduction might wish to look at *Foundations for a Spiritual Education: Research of the Bahá'í Writings*, prepared by the National Bahá'í Education Task Force of the National Spiritual Assembly of the Bahá'ís of the United States.

Chapter 2

1. Personal interview with Christiana Lawson, 24 March 2004.
2. Bahá'u'lláh, *Hidden Words*, Arabic no. 31.
3. Personal interview with Stephen Waite, 1996.
4. Personal interview with Sohayl Mohajer, 1994.
5. Personal interview with Esther Srouji, 1993.
6. Bahá'u'lláh, *Gleanings*, p. 277.
7. ibid. p. 8.
8. ibid. p. 277.
9. Billimoria, *Translating Global Concern into Local Community Programs*, vol. 1, pp. 89–92.
10. See letter written on behalf of Shoghi Effendi to an individual, 5 October 1950, in *Lights of Guidance*, p. 77.
11. Bahá'u'lláh, *Gleanings*, p. 285.

12. Gandhi, from *Young India*, 17 July 1924.
13. Secor, 'The Pragmatist', *Atlantic Monthly*, July/August 2004, p. 44.
14. 'The World This Week', *The Economist*, 31 July – 6 August 2004, p. 8.
15. The Universal House of Justice, *Century of Light*, p. 123.
16. ibid.
17. 'Abdu'l-Bahá, *Paris Talks*, p. 88.
18. ibid. p. 90.
19. From a letter written on behalf of Shoghi Effendi, 14 May 1956, in *High Endeavors*, p. 27.
20. Bahá'u'lláh, *Hidden Words*, Arabic no. 59.
21. ibid. Arabic no. 13.
22. Hitler, *Mein Kampf.*
23. Surowiecki, *Wisdom of Crowds*, p. 34.
24. Bury, *The Invasion of Europe by the Barbarians*, p. 57.
25. Bahá'u'lláh, *Gleanings*, p. 255.
26. National Spiritual Assembly of the Bahá'ís of the United States. *Five Year Plan: 2001–2006 – Junior Youth.*
27. 'In India, a program for rural women emphasizes training as the key to effective use of solar cookers', *One Country*, October – December 2002: http://www.onecountry.org/e143/e14304as_Barli_Solar_story.htm
28. *The Albuquerque Journal*, Saturday, 28 November 1988, p. A2.
29. See, for example, the Calvary Prophecy website: http://www.calvary-prophecy.com/
30. Personal interview with Mojgan Sami, 2004.
31. Anello and Hernández, *Moral Leadership*. This book identifies 18 capabilities that contribute to personal and social relations and improved interpersonal relations.
32. Khadem, 'Blindness Prevention Projects'.

Chapter 3

1. Bahá'u'lláh, *Gleanings*, p. 81.
2. Ahmadiyeh, Talk at Bahá'í Youth Conference, Juarez, Mexico, July 1988.
3. Momen, 'Learning from History', pp. 59–60.
4. ibid. p. 60.
5. Khan, Talk at the Baha'i Centre in Sydney, Australia, 30 November 2003.
6. ibid.

7. Personal interview with Dr Lori Noguchi, 29 October 2003.
8. Shoghi Effendi, *World Order*, p. 42.
9. This was down from 3.3 million in 1996, thanks to a governmental anti-child labour initiative that paid parents to send their children to school. Buckley, 'The Littlest Laborers: Why Does Child Labor Continue to Thrive in the Developing World?' *Washington Post*, 16 March 2000. Reprinted on the Global Policy Forum website, http://www.globalpolicy.org/globaliz/econ/kidlabor.htm
10. Association for the Cohesive Development of the Amazon, Programme Summary, 2002.
11. Personal interview with Mojgan Sami, 2004.
12. Hanson Vick, *Social and Economic Development*, pp. 68–74.
13. Personal interview with Vasu Mohan, 6 March 2004.
14. Personal interview with Mahnaz A. Javid, 19 March 2004.
15. 'Abdu'l-Bahá, *Promulgation*, p. 167.
16. Personal interview with Mahnaz A. Javid, 19 March 2004.
17. Personal interview with Christiana Lawson, 24 March 2004.
18. See Dahl, *The Eco Principle*.
19. Personal interview with Mojgan Sami, 2004.
20. Wally Verderoon, 'Grant Writing 101'.

Chapter 4

1. Momen, 'Learning from History', pp. 65–6.
2. Fukuyama, 'Nation-Building 101', *Atlantic Monthly*, January/February 2004, p. 162.
3. Arbab, 'Promoting a Discourse on Science, Religion, and Development', in *The Lab, the Temple and the Market*, p. 154.
4. Bahá'u'lláh, *Gleanings*, p. 260.
5. From the *Wall Street Journal*, 4 February 1998, p. 1.
6. ibid.
7. *New Straits Times*, Kuala Lumpur, 14 April 2000, quoted in *World Press Review*, June 2000, p. 4.
8. *Bangkok Post*. http://search.bangkokpost.co.th/bkkpost/2000/bp2000_jun/bp20000602/020600_business01.html
9. *Treaty Between the United States of America and the Navajo Tribe of Indians*.
10. ibid.
11. ibid.

12. 'Abdu'l-Bahá, *Promulgation*, pp. 72–3.
13. 'Abdu'l-Bahá, in *Bahá'í World Faith*, p. 406. Parentheses in original.
14. From a postscript to a letter of Shoghi Effendi, 13 April 1927, in *Lights of Guidance*, p. 18.
15. Surowiecki, *Wisdom of Crowds*.
16. This topic is discussed in Hanson Vick, *Social and Economic Development*, pp. 49–60.
17. Discussion between the author and Matt Weinberg, August 2004.
18. Reynolds, 'Home-grown Government', *Aina*, Winter 1996–7, vol. 1, no. 3.
19. Personal interview with Sabine Schuller, 22 December 2003.
20. Personal interview with Nicole Mohajer, 1994.
21. Mehra, 'Leading from the Bottom', *World Press Review*, June 2000, p. 14.
22. Bahá'u'lláh, *Kitáb-i-Aqdas*, para. 30.

Chapter 5

1. Personal interview with Lori Noguchi, 29 October 2003.
2. 'Health for Humanity: It takes a global village . . . to unite around a global vision'.
3. From a letter written on behalf of Shoghi Effendi, 26 October 1949, in *Lights of Guidance*, p. 162.
4. Verderoon, 'Grant Writing 101'.
5. http://www.monafoundation.org/mission.shtml
6. http://www.healthforhumanity.org/
7. ibid. 'Service Delivery vs. Health Development'.
8. Verderoon, 'Grant Writing 101'.
9. ibid.
10. In the United States, board members of non-profit organizations are personally liable for lawsuits against their organizations and organizations need insurance to protect them.
11. Personal Interview with Layli Miller-Muro, 5 December 2003.
12. Ford website: http://www.ford.com/en/company/about/corporate Citizenship/report/principlesRelationshipsWho.htm (last accessed 26 July 2005).
13. Ford website: http://www.ford.com/en/company/about/corporate Citizenship/report/principlesAccountabilityEngagement.htm (last accessed 26 July 2005). Ford adds: 'The proposal was ultimately withdrawn, given the Company's commitment to address HIV/AIDS in

Southern Africa and report on our performance, as well as expand our policies and practices to other global locations.'

14. ibid.
15. One World Trust website: http://www.oneworldtrust.org/?display= project&pid=10 (last accessed 26 July 2005).
16. For an example of an accountability framework that prioritizes stakeholder engagement, see the AccountAbility website: http://www. accountability.org.uk/aa1000/default.asp (last accessed 26 July 2005).
17. Gribbin, *Schrödinger's Kittens*, pp. 200–5.
18. Bahá'í International Community, '. . . *for the betterment of the world*', p. 7.
19. Personal interview with Vasu Mohan, 6 March 2004.
20. ibid.
21. 'Bahá'í Social and Economic Development: Prospects for the Future', in *Readings on Bahá'í Social and Economic Development*, pp. 11, 15.
22. Bahá'í International Community, '. . . *for the betterment of the world*', pp. 6–7.
23. Bahá'í International Community, 'Bahá'í Development Projects: A Global Process of Learning' 2002: http://www.bahai.org/article-1-8-1-1.html (last accessed 15 July 2005).
24. Bahá'í International Community, '. . . *for the betterment of the world*', p. 3.
25. Bahá'u'lláh, *Hidden Words*, Arabic no. 31.
26. 'Bahá'í Social and Economic Development: Prospects for the Future', in *Readings on Bahá'í Social and Economic Development*, p. 13.
27. Personal interview with Vasu Mohan, 6 March 2004.
28. Talk by Jeffrey Hollender, 10 March 2004.
29. ibid.
30. I was assisted in this summary by Vanguard Communications, 'Measuring Outcomes', *Profiles in Communications*, vol. 2, no. 7, July 2003, pp. 1, 3.
31. The United Way website: http://www.unitedway.org/outcomes (last accessed 15 July 2005).
32. Bahá'í International Community, *Valuing Spirituality in Development*, p. 9.
33. Ellison, 'Logic Model Matrix'.
34. For some of the ideas in this section I drew from Sami, 'Measuring Development'.

35. Bahá'í International Community, *Valuing Spirituality in Development*, p. 13.
36. Hanson, 'Global Dilemmas, Local Responses'. http://bahai-library.org/conferences/global.dilemmas.html (last accessed 15 July 2005).
37. Menking, 'Programa Liderazgo Educativo, Ecuador'.
38. Talk by Jeffrey Hollender, 10 March 2004.
39. Diamond, *Collapse*, pp. 446–7.
40. One organization working to incorporate values into businesses is the European Bahá'í Business Forum. This professional association promotes business ethics, corporate social responsibility, sustainable development, partnership of women and men in all fields of endeavour, a new paradigm of work, consultation in decision-making and values-based leadership, according to its website: www.ebbf.org (last accessed 29 July 2005).
41. Vakil, 'Natural Stirrings at the Grassroots: Development, Doctrine, and the Dignity Principle', *Journal of Bahá'í Studies*, vol. 1, no. 2, Feb. 2001, pp. 41–9.
42. The full text of the principles can be found on the website of the International Institute for Sustainable Development, at http://www.iisd.org/measure/principles/bp_full.asp (last accessed 15 July 2005).
43. Bahá'í International Community, '. . . for the betterment of the world', p. 13.
44. ibid.
45. Personal interview with Mahnaz A. Javid, 19 March 2004.
46. Momen, 'A Change of Culture'. Momen explains that part of this decline is due to a stricter definition of who was a Bahá'í but that at the very least it was clear that there had been no growth in the community.
47. Personal interview with Vasu Mohan, 6 March 2004.
48. *Health for Humanity Policy Procedures*.
49. Sami, 'Measuring Development'.
50. ibid.
51. 'Abdu'l-Bahá, in *Compilation*, vol. 1, pp. 508–9, no. 1159.
52. Hanson, 'Global Dilemmas, Local Responses'. http://bahai-library.org/conferences/global.dilemmas.html (last accessed 16 July 2005).
53. Bahá'u'lláh, *Summons of the Lord of Hosts*, para. 179.
54. Personal interview with Mahnaz A. Javid, 19 March 2004.

55. Quoted in Dorsey, 'Positive Deviant', *Fast Company*, December 2000.
56. ibid.
57. Personal interview with Layli Miller-Muro, 5 December 2003.
58. Email from Bill Washington, 18 March 2004.
59. Personal interview with Mahnaz A. Javid, 19 March 2004.
60. Personal interview with Layli Miller-Muro, 5 December 2003.
61. ibid.
62. *Health for Humanity Policy Procedures*.
63. Personal interview with Layli Miller-Muro, 5 December 2003.
64. Personal interview with William Allmost, 2004.
65. Personal interview with Layli Miller-Muro, 5 December 2003.
66. Verderoon, 'Grant Writing 101'.

Chapter 6

1. Bahá'í International Community, '. . . *for the betterment of the world*', p. 5.
2. Personal interview with Lori Noguchi, 29 October 2003.
3. Personal interview with Sabine Schuller, 22 December 2003.
4. Anello and Hernández, *Moral Leadership*.
5. Personal interview with Mahnaz A. Javid, 19 March 2004.
6. Bahá'u'lláh, *Epistle to the Son of the Wolf*, p. 14.
7. Hanson Vick, *Social and Economic Development*, p. 64.
8. Anello and Hernández, *Moral Leadership*.
9. 'Abdu'l-Bahá, *Secret of Divine Civilization*, p. 81.
10. Nabíl-i-A'zam, *Dawn-Breakers*, p. 92.
11. Shoghi Effendi, *Advent of Divine Justice*, p. 50.
12. 'Abdu'l-Bahá, in *Compilation*, vol. 2, p. 338, no. 2052.
13. Gannon, 'Interest in Kabul orphanage wanes, but needy kids remain', Associated Press, 16 November 2002.
14. Verderoon, 'Grant Writing 101'.
15. ISED Solutions, 'Diversifying Agency Funding', *Refugee Assets*, vol. 3, issue 1, March 2004, pp. 1–2.
16. *Health for Humanity 2002 Annual Report*.
17. 'Doing well and doing good', *The Economist*, 31 July – 6 August 2004, pp. 58–9.
18. *Health for Humanity Policy Procedures*.
19. Smith, *Wealth of Nations*, p. 14.

20. 'Abdu'l-Bahá, *Foundations of World Unity*, pp. 43–4.
21. ibid. p. 43.
22. Baha'u'llah, *Tablets*, pp. 132–3.
23. Bahá'u'lláh, *Gleanings*, p. 276.
24. Vakil, 'Natural Stirrings at the Grassroots', in *Journal of Bahá'í Studies*, vol. 11, no. 1, p. 62.
25. National Society of Fundraising Professionals, 'Position Paper: Percentage-Based Compensation'. http://www.nsfre.org/tier3_cd.cfm?folder_id=899&content_item_id=1227
26. Matthew 7:25
27. Kaplan, 'Five Days in Fallujah', *The Atlantic Monthly*, July/August 2004, p. 120.
28. 1 Timothy 6:10
29. This is the MoveOn Political Action Committee, a supporter of liberal politicians in the United States. MoveOn's fundraising success gained the attention of observers of all political leanings.
30. 'Doing well and doing good', *The Economist*, 31 July – 6 August 2004, p. 58. The study is Dale Miller, John Holmes and Melvin Lerner, 'Committing altruism under the cloak of self-interest: the exchange fiction', *Journal of Experimental Social Psychology*, vol. 38.
31. Verderoon, 'Grant Writing 101'.
32. ibid.
33. Personal interview with Soo-Jin Yoon, 2004.
34. ibid.
35. Verderoon, 'Grant Writing 101'.
36. 'Food for Thought for Your Communications Planning', *Profiles in Communications*, vol. 2, no. 7, July 2003.

Chapter 7
1. Bahá'í International Community, '. . . for the betterment of the world', p. 3.
2. World Bank. 'Draft and background papers of the World Bank's Policy Research Report on Gender and Development'. http://www.worldbank.org/gender/prr
3. Gross national income per capita rankings come from the World Bank, World Development Indicators database, September 2004: http://www.worldbank.org/data/quickreference/quickref.html. The corruption rankings are from Transparency International, *Global Corruption*

     Report 2003: http://www.globalcorruptionreport.org/gcr2003.htm
4. Gandhi, from *Young India*, 17 July 1924.
5. Gandhi, from *Diary of Mahadev Desai*.
6. Personal interview with Vasu Mohan, 6 March 2004.
7. Personal interviews with Sohayl Mohajer, 1994.
8. Personal interview with Lori Noguchi, 29 October 2003.
9. Bahá'í International Community, *Valuing Spirituality in Development*, p. 6.
10. ibid. pp. 6–7.
11. ibid. p. 14.
12. ibid. pp. 14–18.
13. Davis and Maghzi, 'Learning about the Application of Principle-Based Indicators of Development'.
14. Hanson, 'Global Dilemmas, Local Responses'. http://bahai-library.org/conferences/global.dilemmas.html
15. 'Abdu'l-Bahá, *Promulgation*, p. 239.
16. Bahá'u'lláh, *Kitáb-i-Aqdas*, p. 91.
17. Personal interview with Vasu Mohan, 6 March 2004.
18. The Barefoot Artists website. http://www.barefootartists.org/index.html (last accessed 17 August 2005).
19. Beckett, *Sister Wendy's Story of Painting*, p. 60.
20. ibid. p. 259.
21. Bahá'u'lláh, *Kitáb-i-Aqdas*, para. 51.
22. Letter from the Universal House of Justice to the Followers of Bahá'u'lláh in the Cradle of the Faith, the Day of the Covenant, 26 November 2003.
23. 'Abdu'l-Bahá, *Promulgation*, p. 169.
24. Carlson, 'Study shows that genes can protect kids against poverty'. http://www.news.wisc.edu/9853.html

Chapter 8

1. Diamond, *Collapse*, p. 495.
2. Worldwatch Institute, *State of the World* 2003, p. 5.
3. Bahá'u'lláh, *Hidden Words*, Arabic no. 2.
4. Bahá'u'lláh, *Tablets*, p. 157.
5. Bahá'u'lláh, *Kitáb-i-Íqán*, p. 31.
6. Raghavan, 'UN officials stunned to find refugee camp emptied in

Sudan', *Chicago Tribune*, 2 July 2004; and Wax, 'In Sudan, Death and Denial: Officials Accused of Concealing Crisis as Thousands Starve', *Chicago Tribune*, 27 June 2004, p. A1.

7. Welch, 'California Rules, Detroit Quakes', *BusinessWeek*, 12 July 2004, pp. 36–7.

8. Quoted in Kahane, *Logic and Contemporary Rhetoric*, p. 111.

9. This isn't meant to downplay the importance of branding. Coca-Cola outpaced what had been the world's most popular soft drink, Moxie, because it invested in advertising while the Moxie Company spent its marketing money buying sugar. The difference is that while Coke was building its brand, it also knew it had a business plan for making money.

10. Keats, 'Copy This Article and Win Quick Cash!' *Wired*, issue 12.07, July 2004.

11. See 'Reproduction and Other Biological Subjects'. http://bahai-library.com/?file=uhj_reproduction.html; and a letter of the Universal House of Justice to an individual, 23 August 2001. http://bahai-library.com/uhj/stem.cells.html

12. From a letter written on behalf of the Universal House of Justice to an individual, 5 June 1988. http://bahai-library.com/?file=uhj_legislating_morality.html

13. John 8:31–2

14. Anello and Hernández, *Moral Leadership*.

15. Bahá'u'lláh, *Epistle to the Son of the Wolf*, p. 93.

16. Some of the arguments above are adapted from Lairson and Skidmore, *International Political Economy: The Struggle for Power and Wealth*, pp. 259–61.

17. Hirsh, 'What are We Fighting For?' *Newsweek*, 24 April 2000.

18. Klein, 'Baghdad Year Zero', *Harper's Magazine*, September 2004, p. 47.

19. Pink, 'The New Face of the Silicon Age', *Wired*, February 2004, pp. 98, 101.

20. Hussein, 'Dimensions of independent socio-economic development', Muslimedia International, July 2004. http://www.muslimedia.com/socioecon-adil.htm

21. Nagaratnam, in *The Heart of the Lotus*.

22. LaFraniere, 'Cellphones Catapult Rural Africa to 21st Century', *New York Times*, 25 August 2005. http://www.nytimes.com/2005/08/25/international/africa/25africa.html (last accessed 26 August 2005).

23. Friedman, *The Lexus and the Olive Tree*, p. 360.
24. Langewiesche, 'The Accuser', *The Atlantic Monthly*, March 2005, p. 72.
25. *Encyclopaedia Britannica*.
    http://www.1911encyclopedia.org/F/FE/FERRARA_FLORENCE_COUNCIL_OF.htm. The rift is also explained in the *Catholic Encyclopedia*, http://www.newadvent.org/cathen/06111a.htm
26. Johnson, Hannon and Sister M. Dominica, *The Story of the Church*, p. 158.
27. Prophet Muhammad's Charter of Privileges, 628 AD. http://www.cyberistan.org/islamic/charter1.html (last accessed 26 August 2005).
28. Based on Grayzel, *History of the Jews*, pp. 236–7.
29. Shoghi Effendi, *Advent of Divine Justice*, p. 40.
30. Schoonmaker, 'Revisioning the Women's Movement', *Circle of Unity*.
31. Namazie, 'Saying no', iranian.com (last accessed 12 October 2004).
32. UNHCR, '2003: The Year in Review'. *Refugees*, vol. 4, p. 133.
33. 'Abdu'l-Bahá, *'Abdu'l-Bahá in London*, p. 29.
34. Baha'u'llah, *Tablets*, p. 264.
35. Locke, 'Second Treatise on Government', chapter 2.
36. ibid.
37. Bahá'u'lláh, *Gleanings*, p. 247.
38. Battistella, 'The Human Rights of Migrants: A Pastoral Challenge', *Migration, Religious Experience, and Globalization*, p. 92.
39. 'Publius', cited in Cohen and Fermon, 'The Federalist Papers', *Princeton Readings in Political Thought*, no. 51. See also http://www.foundingfathers.info/federalistpapers/fedindex.htm (last accessed 14 August 2005).
40. Vakil, 'Natural Stirrings at the Grassroots: Development, Doctrine, and the Dignity Principle', *Journal of Bahá'í Studies*, vol. 11, no.1, February 2001, p. 44.
41. 'Abdu'l-Bahá, *Promulgation*, p. 175.
42. Momen, 'Reformulating the Bahá'í Faith: An Approach to Teaching Chinese Peoples'.
43. Bahá'u'lláh, *Kitáb-i-Aqdas*, para. 125.
44. The Universal House of Justice, *Individual Rights and Freedoms in the World Order of Bahá'u'lláh*, para, 51.
45. Smee, 'Women end 19-year anti-nuclear protest', *USA Today*, 6 September 2000, p. 13A.
46. 'Abdu'l-Bahá, *Promulgation*, p. 135.